DATE DUE

OC 20 '98			
DE 18 '98			
OC 19 '99			

DEMCO 38-296

BLACKS IN CORRECTIONS
Understanding Network Systems
In Prison Society

Clyde E. DeBerry

 Wyndham Hall Press

ECTIONS:
Understanding Network Systems
In Prison Society

by Clyde E. DeBerry

International Standard Book Number

1-55605-241-3 (paper)
1-55605-242-1 (cloth)

Printed in the United States of America

Wyndham Hall Press
Bristol, IN   46507-9460

Dedication to loving memory of my parents Wayne and Josephine DeBerry whose respect, devotion, and the "hang on in there" attitude continue to serve as a motivator factor to me.

To me sister, Betty DeBerry-Lenior has been a wise, caring and concerned young sister.

To all of my kinfolk that I have enjoyed family reunions, funerals and small get-to-gathers over many years. I always have and continue to appreciate and love you all.

ACKNOWLEDGMENTS

It is not possible to acknowledge the help of all who have contributed to this book. Some folks stand out in my mind because of their encouragement in the past as well as in the "here and now".

I am grateful to Dr. P. Ray Kedia, Head of the Department of Criminal Justice and Dr. Dardanella Ennis, Dean of College of Liberal Arts here at Grambling State University for affording me the opportunity to complete this book. I appreciate Dr. Billy Williams, Professor of Criminal Justice, for his critical comments. Particular thanks to Drs. Nathan and Julia Hare, for their encouragement, advice and comments that made this a much better book. They are a team that understands from the 1960's struggle, and thereafter what networking really means in the real sense of the word. Dr. Hare was the first person hired to coordinate a Black Studies program in the United States. I especially thank Dr. Robert E. Agger, former Professor of Political Science, University of Oregon, for his academic guidance throughout my graduate program at U. of O., and for his brilliant analysis of complex political issues. He was not only my mentor but a good colleague and a friend.

I am deeply indebted to a few correctional facilities, as well as the staff, for their unselfish time and advise assisting me with providing psychological services offender populations.

I would also like to express my appreciation to those offenders in corrections that helped me with questionnaires and those who actually participated in the study, for without offenders there would be no story. I am very appreciative of Dr. John Morgan, President of Wyndham Hall Press, who offered many valuable suggestions regarding style and content. I would like to further extend my thanks to Mrs. Veronica Adams-Cooper who typed from draft to disk. Of course, all responsibility of content and point of view are my own.

My thanks to my wife Elaine, and to my two sons, Mikio and Yaphet and the little grandson, Kwamme for their consideration, patience and cooperation while this project was in progress.

A LUTA CONTINUE - LASIMA THUSHINDE MBILISHAKA (The struggle will continue and we will conquer without a doubt).

May 1, 1994
Clyde E. DeBerry

**A Message to Readers, Students, Correctional Staff,
and All Interested Community Folks**

There is an old African proverb that suggests, it is the community's responsibility to rear its own children. In a real sense this means, it is not only the parents' responsibility, it is also the church, the school, YMCA, an extended family, the family next door, across and down the street, and etc. Every person and institution in the community has a hand in that child's social interest, which will help him or her belong to the human community. The break down of community responsibility to its children is part and parcel of some of the reasons correctional facilities are overcrowded with young folks.

The Sentencing Project released a study at the end of 1990 that reported that the United States has achieved the highest known rate of incarceration with 426 jail and prison inmates per 100,000 and the now-defunct Soviet Union recorded 268 per 100,000. With a 1990 federal and state prison population in excess of 704,000 inmates, the decade of the 1980's experienced a 113 percent increase (from 329,821 in 1980) in the number of offenders confined (Bureau of Justice Statistics, 1990a). The percentage of increase in 1989 alone was 12 percent and added over 76,000 prisoners to the nation's prison population. Based on Bureau of Justice Statistics figures, an additional 1,500 new prison beds per week (1990a).

While these figures represent record-high levels for incarcerated offenders, the increase in the number of offenders supervised in the community has also been phenomenal. The Bureau of Justice Statistics reported that more than three million offenders were on probation and parole at the end of 1990 - 2,670,234 on probation and 531,407 on parole (1991). Since 1980, this represents a 126 percent increase in the probation population and 107 percent increase in the parole population.

These population figures indicate that since the end of 1980, when approximately 1.8 million persons were under some form of correctional control and supervision, to the end of 1989 when the number had increased to 4.1 million - 1 out of every 46 adults were in correctional facilities. The number of offenders has grown beyond a capacity as public policies have expanded the scope of social control, [*reflecting both the public's fear of crime and the politician's fear of reform-crime policy which has been consistent with a conservative agenda that has focused on deterrence, incapacitation, and punishment.*] And while some contend that there is "no relationship between the incarceration rate and violent crime" (O'Brien cited in Malcolm, 1991: B16), the growing number of prisoners is becoming its own issue and a major corrections dilemma.

As the annual cost of incarceration policies reaches $16 billion (The Sentencing Project, 1990), economic pressures begin to create their own realities. Commenting on these overwhelming costs, Kenneth McGinnis, Director of the Department of Corrections in Illinois, observed that "prisons will simply bankrupt the states unless we find cheaper ways to punish and figure out how to keep all these people from returning" (cited in Malcolm, 1991).

[In order to dramatically reduce crime by the year 2000, it will take much stronger and highly organized community network system, this system must consist of communicating, associating, and the education, both those youths outside and inside our correctional institutions.] We must look at a few other issues that impinge upon the seriousness of the reintegration process for our correction populations in the U.S.

One of the best kept secrets by media is that recent studies indicate urban city blacks are decreasing their use of certain drugs. This finding certainly indicates there is some networking taking place in urban America. This trend may lead to reduction of not only substance abuse but also criminal or antisocial behaviors. Examples of excellent current networking are major studies which show Black youth having the lowest rates of use for virtually all drugs - licit and illicit. While this image of Black youth as disciplined non-drug users runs counter to headline and TV reports, let's look at the facts.

-Smoking: In 1976, about 38% of both White and Black high school seniors smoked; in 1992 about 32% of White seniors smoked, but only 8.2% of Blacks, (U.S. Surgeon General's Report 1994).

-Cocaine and crack: In 1986, 13.5% of White seniors used cocaine, compared to 5.8% of Blacks. Presently, 0.8% of Black seniors use, compared to 3.1% Whites.

-Alcohol: About 32% of White seniors are heavy drinkers, compared to 11% of Black seniors, reported by the University of Michigan's Monitoring the Future Project.

These low numbers hold despite higher school dropout rates for Blacks. The smoking decline comes amid intense cigarette ads in Black areas and as more inner-city stores illegally sell loose cigarettes, a subject in the February 25, 1994, issue of the Journal of the American Medical Association.

What explains this secular trend? On smoking, experts have cited rising cigarette costs, anti-smoking ads and a pro-health attitude. On drugs, they cited the ads, such as the one equating drug use with frying your brain, and a heightened awareness of the risks of drugs and resulting violence in the inner city.

Another strong factor is that Black youth are more committed to religion and more likely to belong to strict fundamentalist denominations. Ministers and educators who are preaching against drugs and putting in anti-drug programs shouldn't stop. However, churches cannot do it alone. The job of keeping our youth from going to prison falls on all of us. Churches, businesses, civic and social groups all have a role in networking with our youth.

There are winners and losers in the numbers game of what is working and what is not for our youth. We believe that networking is the key to rescuing a generation some say that is already lost: lost to drugs, lost to gangs and violence, lost to teen pregnancy, lost to prisons, and lost to the cemeteries.

This may sound reasonable but we must create an environment where people can survive. New careers for urban Blacks must be of high priority. To re-educate a young urban Black about "going straight" either in prison or out of prison when there is little likelihood for employment for him is throwing fuel on the fire. Training opportunities must also be high on the list. Provided we are serious about criminal behavior, nowadays, training and employment must go hand in hand. The educational training must not only be in traditional academia and vocational types. It must include education on drugs, morals and civil disobedience, networking, and play and work. We must deal in our relations with urban youth and offenders from multi-dimensional, reality perspectives and not a single dimension perspective. A single dimension with urban youth would lead us like in the past to tunnel vision with limited options toward success.

The multi-dimensional perspective will have to involve a number of network systems, working cooperatively with each other to have an impact on the lives of all "imprisoned persons" whether they are urban, community and/or prison youths.

This manuscript lends itself toward understanding the network system of prison society in corrections. It was conceived as an experimental handbook for advanced undergraduate and graduate students in social and behavioral sciences and particularly those in the areas of criminal justice. Several unique advantages arise from presenting individual chapters as separate headings rather than under a single topic. Each chapter was written by the author as building units based upon research obtained in the study. New chapters eventually can be added, as information becomes available, particularly regarding controversial areas and individual chapters can be revised independently. Finally, to a degree, an instructor of advanced courses in social and behavioral science can choose a particular set of chapters or topics to meet the needs of his or her students.

Probably the most important impetus for this handbook comes from the fact that a suitable book did not exist for students at Grambling State University that dealt with the psychology of Blacks in correctional systems and staff reactions toward that system.

This book is written for any student or person who wants to understand some of the conceptual and empirical knowledge behind that information and advice. It is a research project on the psychological attitudes of prison offenders as they seek help in forming network systems in and out of their society. The book also deals with urban community network system that is often times a spin off in corrections.

The theoretical discussion itself is reasonably comprehensive, eclectic, somewhat non-controversial, and apolitical. But the research and examples are not. They are presented as expressed by the offenders to illustrate how personal and political considerations become not only relevant but unavoidable when the scientist travels from his or her conceptual and empirical *knowledge to this advice, when the travels from Blacks in correction to a Black on college campus.*

Thus, the empirical presentations in this handbook should not make it unmistakably a personal essay. Unlike most examples in handbooks, those here are more than pedagogical aids to understanding. They are the real black eye peas with pork-meat which gives the peas their flavor and, let us hope, make it worth the eating.

TABLE OF CONTENTS

CHAPTER ONE

INTRODUCTION

BLACKS IN CORRECTIONS:
Theoretical Considerations for Crime and the Network System

One of the most formidable problems facing American society today is crime. Crime is not a new phenomenon and indeed has been characterized by some as "an American way of life." What is new about crime is that it is only now beginning to be scrutinized by the masses of people because of its growth and complexity, its destructive effects on national life and its psychologically, socially and economically damaging effects.

"Violent crime and the fear it provokes are crippling our society, limiting personal freedom and fraying the ties that bind us," said President Bill Clinton in his State of the Union Address on January 25, 1994.

The President is right. For most Americans, particularly Blacks in America, crime has become the number one problem facing their communities. Parents are frightened about the safety of their children. Kids worry about being shot in the corridors of their schools by a classmate with a gun. Neighbors patrol urban streets but still cannot protect themselves and their loved ones from drive-by shootings by gang members. Those who have enough money search for safe places to live and find that these havens no longer exist. Every citizen is hostage to the fear that he or she may be shot on a commuter train or in a fast-food restaurant by a deranged person.

We believe that something must be done to stop this tide of violent crime in America. Already some states and local organizations are working together on ways to combat crime. The federal Crime Bill passed in the fall of 1993 by the Senate has prodded national politicians and policy makers to think creatively about this important issue. All agree that it will take a concerted effort to win the war against crime. This is among a number of reasons why we wish to study and understand behaviors of Blacks in Corrections. This writer believes that by studying and understanding Blacks in the prisons systems, we may learn how to keep persons out of correctional systems.

This notion will take a concerted effort on the part of all its community people. In a sense, this is what we mean by social networking. Various community persons, social groups and organizations will have to pool and network their resources to win the war on crime, thereby keeping young people out of prison, and at the same time, developing a network system with those in prisons so that once out of "low bonds" they can remain crime-free. We must help the very young people and our youth to develop social interest within the context of the network system. Having social interest helps to manage their lives and at some time make a contribution to our community. Social interest means having self-worth.

What forms the personality of a human being? What makes an individual act, criminal acts, he/she does? What forces govern all the activities of the human mind including the criminal mind? These are the fundamental questions which criminal psychology tries to answer. So many people are now exploring them and there are so many theories that we are apt to become confused. Some assume that the life of each individual is determined by the experience and desires of his ancestors. Others regard the psyche as the battlefield of a variety of instincts, corresponding to various forms of the sexual instinct. Many think that the most complicated behavior patterns are the outcome of the automatic action of certain reflex mechanisms, which are built up and maintained by habit. Other look upon many with all his functions as the mere product of his environment, which through the medium of education directs his behavior. A number of other theories have been advanced by different pioneers in order to explain the psychic paranormal phenomena. The leading idea of the Individual Psychology of Alfred Adler is found in his recognition of the importance of human society, not only for the development of the individual character, but also for the orientation of every single action and emotion in the life of a human being.

Most of us have no adequate idea of the extent to which people nowadays depend on cooperation with other people. This notion also refers to the criminal. We only have to think of the thousands of people who labor we employ each day, or need only consider how many people cooperate to provide our houses, clothing, food, and a thousand other necessities of our daily lives. For thousands of years man has lived in more or less close social relation with his fellow man and has adapted himself to a system of division of labor and mutual assistance. The human infant is one of the most defenseless creatures in the world. He cannot find his food without help, or even move alone. In exercising all his functions, he depends on the cooperation of others.

The question now arises: to what extent can living in a closely knit community form the character of an individual. It might seem as Freud maintains, that human instincts adapt themselves only incompletely and faultily to the reality of close social relationships and that the human psyche is indeed at the mercy of incompatible demands--the need for adjustment to the community, and the needs of instincts. Observation shows that not only among people, but also among animals, close social relationships, with the very delicate adjustment to the claim of others which is involved in such relationships, decisively effect the nature and characteristics of species, and even enable some individuals to free themselves from the laws of nature which otherwise prove generally irresistible, and actions of an individual are determined by the experiences he encounters in the community within which he grows up. According to Adler, we are a mere product of our environment. This frame of reference includes the environment of criminal and non-criminal worlds. If we look deeper we find that in addition to the influence of environment, another vitally important circumstance remains to be considered. Different people respond in different ways to the same experience and influences. We do not merely react. We adopt an individual attitude. The attitude adopted depends on the impressions the individual forms in early childhood. Environment is indeed a forceful factor. Yet this environment is not the individual's real environment, but merely his environment as it appears subjectively to him. This concept tends to appear as to why criminals view the world differently than non-criminals. Therefore, the decisive factor for the development of character is not the influence of environment, but the attitude to environment which the individual takes up. We develop our characteristic behavior--our character-- by opposition or support, negation or affirmation, acceptance or non-acceptance of the group into which we are born.

Our urges to adapt ourselves to the arbitrary conditions of our environment is expressed by the social interest innate in every human being. But this innate social characteristic, which is common to all, must be developed if the individual is to be qualified to fulfill the complicated demands of the community in which the civilized adult lives. However, criminals' social interest remains underdeveloped. This may be one of the reasons why they are unable to meet the expected demands of their environments.

Dr. Alfred Adler also stated, that the human community sets three tasks for every individual. They are: 1) Work, which means contributing to the welfare of others, 2) Friendship, which means embracing social relationships with friends, peers, and relatives, and 3) Love, which is participating in the most intimate union with someone of the other sex and represents the strongest and closest emotional relationship with can exist between two human beings.

These three tasks embrace the whole of human life with all its desires and activities. All human suffering originates from difficulties which complicate the task. The possibility of fulfilling them does not depend on the individual's talents nor on his intelligence. People of outstanding capacity fail where others with far inferior powers achieve relative success. It all depends on social interest. The better this is developed and the happier the relationship between the individual and the human community, the more successfully does he fulfill the three life tasks, and the better balanced his character and personality appear. Most individuals we have met in the prison environment were at least deficient in one or more of these tasks.

Social interest is expressed subjectively in the consciousness of having something in common with other people and of "being one of them." People can develop their capacity for cooperation only if they feel that in spite of all external dissimilarities they are not fundamentally different from other people--if they feel belonging. A person's ability to cooperate may therefore be regarded as a measure of the development of his social interest. In our relations with men behind the bars, their life stories were one of competition rather than cooperation. It is the former that lead to their defeat and the lack of self-worth.

We certainly want to do what we can to help find a society embracing the whole human race, to whose interest all the special interest of individuals and groups would be subordinated. But in practice we are still a long way from realizing this ideal. The social interest, is the key to social network, for balance living has no fixed objectives. Much more truly may it be said to create an attitude towards life, a desire to cooperate with others in some way and to master the situations of life. Social interest is the expression of our capacity for give and take in a social network system.

This pilot study sought to identify various types of social network support systems and that of social interest among Maximum Security Prison Offenders and also to examine the relationship between social networks, social well-being, network satisfaction, and attitudes toward seeking professional help for emotional problems.

We will discuss as follows:

1.   What type of support/help do prison offenders utilize within their social network?
     a.   Nature and extent of social network
     b.   Supports available
     c.   Level of satisfaction with supports

2.   Does the attitude of the social network influence the individual's decision to seek professional help for personal problems?

3.   What factors influence a person's decision to seek professional help?

4.   What type of problems cause people to seek professional help?

In order to ascertain whether a correlation exists between social network support and social well-being, a separate measure of social well-being was generated, using a scale developed by Donald and Ware (1982).

It should be clearly stated from the outset that a great deal of the review of literature from non-prison population is not quoted because of limited availability of research information in the area of prison study on network and psychological attitudes among offenders. For the time-being we have found that much of the literature referring to non-prison population can apply to our initial understanding of prison population.

As most of you well know at the present time, there is little or no research information available on Black social networks and cultural factors that may influence the individual's decision to seek prison or non-prison mental health services. In the past, the extended family system and the Black church have been two traditional cultural entities that have provided support, psychological security, and assistance to Black Americans during times of crisis. A prison offender does have access to family, ministers and church members unless he or she refused visits from them.

One hundred and ten adult offenders were administered a 30-item questionnaire designed to measure social well-being, network utilization for emotional problems, and network satisfaction. Correlational analysis was utilized to examine the relationship between the three variables.

Results indicated that among these offenders social well-being was highly interrelated with network satisfaction and network utilization for emotional problems. An interrelationship was also found between social network satisfaction and use of network solving for psychological problems.

Factors that contributed to the decision to seek professional services will be identified, as well as those factors that interfered with the utilization of services.

Implication for the development of treatment modalities and public policy sensitive to the Black offenders' needs will be addressed, as well as recommendations for future research for social change.

In conclusion, the most potent weapon against crime is intelligent and realistic prevention. In order to prevent a problem or find a solution to it, the issue relevant to that problem must first be understood.

CHAPTER TWO

DESCRIPTION AND DEFINITION OF SOCIAL
NETWORK SYSTEMS IN PRISON/URBAN SETTINGS

A lengthy search was conducted of the literature specifically centered around linkages or social network with Blacks in the U.S.A. prison population. Only one source was located.

Swan (1983) described and identified a composite of Black prisoners' families and determined the nature and extent of adjustment, economic, and related problems these families faced before, during and after the imprisonment of a family member. This study concluded that the major problem facing Black prisoners and their families both before and during imprisonment was a lack of adequate finances.

In today's world, finances seem to be a serious problem of non-prison Blacks as well as for those in prison. It has been suggested by some Black social scientists that it is the lack of opportunity for financial independence that leads or allows many young Blacks to choose crime as part of their lifestyle which further promotes the dilemma in prison settings.

In examining social network systems, concentration is focused on non-prison environments data in order to understand it further and employ it in prison environments among Blacks.

A social network may be defined as a group of people with a common link. It can consist of groups such as one's immediate family, relatives, friends, neighbors, work associates, social club acquaintances, and even prison members. It can serve as an enduring support system and act as a buffer against psychological problems. The social network model was originally developed from sociological and anthropological studies of kinship groups. Barnes (1954), a British anthropologist, first identified the term "third field" to describe the social relations of extended kin, friends, and other social contacts (Bott, 1970, p. 324). The model has also begun to be utilized by psychologists who are interested in conceptualizing human behavior in the context of family and social systems. Bott (1970) states that:

> Social network is the sort of concept that can be used in many conceptual frames of reference. It has been used in conjunction with traditional structural functional theory in the analysis of societies and groups as open systems and in conjunction with situational analysis, sociological theory and the construction of generative models. (P. 330)

Social network theory and concepts are essential to any study where focus is on the way in which social relations link and divide individuals and group within a specific location or social category. This would be specifically among isolated prison populations. According to Bott, there are three types of studies that can only be formulated by using constructs from network theory. They are: studies of system environment which explain the impact of the environment on social relations, studies of social process, and the generating of social norms. The present study among Blacks falls under the category of studies on social linkage and is concerned with the by-products of the social interactions.

Dean and Linn (1977) identify seven characteristic interactions that exist in the social network of the nuclear family or primary kin group. They are the emphasis on mutual responsibility; caring and concern; strong mutual identification; emphasis on the person as a unique individual rather than on his or her performance; face-to-face interaction and communication; intimacy, close association; and provision for support, affection, security and response.

The work of Mitchell and Trickett (1980) further expands the knowledge of social networks. They list three major components crucial to the analysis os social networks: structural characteristics of networks refer to their size and range, the number of people the individual has contact with, the frequency of contact, geographic distance, and years of residence. Network density refers to the average number of relationships each member has with others in the same network. The normative context of the relationship refers to those groupings of individuals who comprise the social networks, such as the primary kin, secondary kin, or extended family, friends, neighbors, and work acquaintances.

The term "Natural Social Network" is used by Turkat (1980) to distinguish friends, significant associates and family who provide housing, financial assistance, critical information, encouragement, and guidance during a time of crisis.

The present prison study focused on the frequency of contact with four social network groups: family, friends, neighbors, and voluntary organizations, and the type of support and assistance they provide in prison.

SOCIAL NETWORKS AND PSYCHOLOGICAL ADAPTION

Social scientists have long assumed that an individual's social support system may help to mediate or buffer the effect of negative life crisis on psychological adaptation. Research studies to date indicate signs of this relationship; however, no conclusive evidence has been found. This appears to be due primarily to methodological weakness and limited application. How social networks respond or become mobilized during a life crisis or event has been described by Boswell (1969), and Walker, et al. (1977). The Boswell study focused on rural social relations in Central Africa. He was particularly concerned with the way individuals deal with the immediate crisis situation in which they find themselves. The author tells in detail how the crisis of bereavement is handled in the village of Lusaka. Relatives and friends closest to the deceased kin gather at the house of the deceased and contribute to the collection of money, preparing of food, and planning funeral arrangements. The closest kin takes charge at the mortuary. Depending on the sex of the deceased, male or female kinsmen prepare the body for burial. The village senior kinsmen will recount to those who are unable to come to town how the death took place, funeral arrangements, and the mourning process.

During the past six months, two Black offenders died from cancer. It was observed by this writer that large numbers of Black offenders took on a personal caring and grieving toward both the dying offenders and their families. In fact, before the deaths of the two offenders' some offenders arranged for other offenders to stay in contact with the families as a supportive group and after the two offenders deaths the offenders designed, signed and delivered a large card bearing their regrets.

Walker, et al. (1977), also wrote on change in the role of social networks during the crisis of bereavement. According to the authors, three factors influence the type of needs most salient to a person in crisis:

1.   First, the nature of the crisis. A crisis as severe illness does not necessarily involve a major role change or loss of person support such as that found in the loss of a spouse.

2.   The second factor in determining the most appropriated type of support is time. A person's needs can change and thus network structures which fulfill certain needs at the onset of crisis may become maladaptive during a later stage in the transition process.

3.   A third group of factors involves the internal and external resources of the individual in crisis. For example, if the individual's personality structure is not receptive to making use of network supports or information, of if the physical situation does not allow mobility to follow through on such contacts, then the network will be of little utility. (p. 38)

Practical application of network concepts to the crisis of bereavement were also suggested. They include the organization of a widow's support group with widows providing "informal caregiving." Persons may be given the names and phone numbers of those who are willing to help. The widow's contact can serve as a strong emotionally supportive tie during the early stage of bereavement, and later to bridge or facilitate a transition into a single existence.

The research of Andres, et al. (1978) and Linn, et al. (1977), report a positive association between social support and psychological well-being. The Andrews study interviewed 863 residents of an Australian suburb. Support was defined in three ways: direct crisis support (the number of people available to help), indirect support from neighbors (number and direction of ties in the community), and indirect support from social organizations. A life events inventory and general health questionnaire were used to measure the level of life stress and psychological impairment. Direct crisis support was found to be the only type of support that differentiated the psychologically impaired respondents from the non-impaired. The Linn study involved 160 Chinese-American adults living in Washington, D.C. Social support was measured by utilizing a 9-item scale which tapped the respondent's interactions and involvement with friends, neighbors, family, and community. Results revealed that social support and stressful life events are important factors in explaining psychiatric symptoms. A very weak mediating effect was found between social support, stressors, and illness. As in the Andrews study, social support was found to have some positive effect on psychological well-being.

A study of the effects of social support on psychological adaptation in a clinical population was initiated by Turner (1979). He investigated the support system of 103 formerly hospitalized schizophrenics from a poor rural county. Support was defined in terms of having confidants, any level of satisfaction within the support system, and experiencing no stigma within the community. The higher functioning respondents were more satisfied with their supports, and also had more non-familial network contacts. Unfortunately, the study was not able to differentiate the effects of emotional support from the sense of stigma. However, it did initiate a relationship between lack of support and serious psychological disorder.

Williams, et al. (1981), conducted a longitudinal study on the role of social support to the adjustment of life events and mental health. They examined whether social supports benefit mental health only in a direct manner or interact to modify effects of stressful events. Two research models were designed; an additive model in which life events and social supports each have a direct independent effect on mental health, and a model with additive and interactive effects. The additive/interactive model states that social contacts and resources have a stress modifying or buffering role on life events. Data were gathered from 2,234 persons living in Seattle. All respondents were enrolled in the Rand Health Insurance Experiment, which examined the effect of health care financing on utilization of health services. The results of the study support the following conclusions:

> 1) Social supports predict improvements in mental health over time. 2) Life events and physical limitations predict a deterioration in mental health over time. 3) The negative effects of life events and physical limitations on mental health do not vary according to the amount of social support. 4) Differences in the measurement strategies for life events and social supports produce some variance in results, but not in conclusion about whether effects on mental health are additive or interactive. (Williams, et al., p. 324)

Thoits (1982) reviews the previously mentioned research and other empirical literature in her study of "Social Support as a Buffer Against Life Stress." The author identifies three methodological problems that have limited the general ability of research findings. First, most studies suffer from inadequate conceptualization and operationalization of the concept of social support. Second, the majority of the studies either theoretically or operationally confounded the direct effect of life events with the buffering or interactive effect. Third, most researchers have failed to examine the theoretically pertinent and practically significant main effect of social support upon distress.

Thoits offers the following solutions to the identified problems. First, that investigators formulate precise conceptual definitions of social support and reliable indicators of the concept. Imprecise conceptualizations can result in invalid operationalizations. Second, clear distinction must be made between when and how social support is measured before, after, or independently of a life stress or change. If this is not accomplished, the results will be biased toward the "buffering" hypothesis. A longitudinal study would appear to be the best measure of this relationship. Finally, the relationships between social support, life events, and psychological state must be a hypothesis derived from theory instead of empirical generalizations.

Leavy (1983) follows the work of Thoits in providing a critical review of empirical research on social support and psychological disorder. He identifies similar problems in methodology and conceptualization, along with the need for reliability in measures and an over-reliance on retrospective designs.

The author also provides the following summary and discussion of major findings:

> 1.   The absence of social supports is associated with increased psychological distress. This pattern is clearly seen in schizophrenics who frequently have no support. The pattern is similar but less dramatic for non-psychotic disorders. At the present, no assertion can be made as to the minimum number of supportive relationships which correlate with psychological health or adaptation. It appears that one source of emotional support may be necessary and sufficient in some cases, while more support is needed in others.
>
> 2.   Evidence shows that variables other than size are involved in the support/coping dimension. The composition of the network is crucial, along with the reciprocity of support activities. Future research should examine related network character-istics.
>
> 3.   The type of support that people receive is a central factor related to psychological adaptation. Emotional support is seen as a correlate of emo-tional health. Community attachments may provide a specialized source of support. This appears to be especially important to ethnic groups.
>
> 4.   The amount and type of support received must also take into account the quality of support; i.e., it is better to have a small network with quality than a large network with inadequate support. Dissatisfaction with support correlates with a variety

of psychological problems. Rather than assuming there is one ideal type of support, research should include the respondents' description of "high-quality support." Real/ideal differences may predict or account for psychological distress better than measures of actual supports.

BLACKS AND SOCIAL NETWORK SYSTEMS

Social networks within the Black community function to assist members in meeting emotional and financial needs while also providing them with sources of identity and helping to buffer against the many deplorable effects of racism. The majority of research on Blacks and social networks has focused on the family and extended kinship system.

E. Franklin Frazier's classic work on "The Negro Family in the United State" (1939) outlines the problems, strengths and cultural traditions unique to the development of Black families from slavery to the 20th Century. He describes the strategic position and dominant role held by the slave mother during the plantation years. The matrilineal system developed because fathers were taken away from children before birth. Male elders and other male extended family members therefore played an important role in the children's development and in the survival of the family system.

Strong kinship bonds is one of the five traits which Hill (1972) identified as contributing to Black survival. The others include flexibility of role, high achievement orientation, strong work orientation and strong religious orientation. In this same vein, Nobles (1975) suggests that the strength and stability of the Black family has been influenced by certain traits or Africanisms that have been retained in Black culture. He states that various African cosmological concepts such as a sense of "oneness" of being and the nature of being as force and spirit implies that the family is the center of the universe. This view of the family as the center of the universe helps to strengthen ties to an extended kin group. Staples (1978) goes on to describe the important role and functioning of the extended kin group in the socialization of children. Many Black adults often speak of being "raised" by their grandmother or other family elders. Staples explains that:

> Despite a host of negative assumptions about the ability of Black families to produce children with a healthy identity, we find that traditionally the extended family system had a number of mothering figures for a child. This is in contrast to a number of middle class white children who are prisoners of the nuclear family system. Either they receive love and approval from their parents or not at all. In general, Black children develop a healthy identity because they grow up in households where they experience love and security from a number of kinsmen and significant others, and are not stifled by the rigidity of age, and sex roles which exclude them from family activities. (p. 89)

The extended kinship group can be comprised of blood relations along with close friends who become part of the family. Sociologists and anthropologists use the term pseudokin to describe friends who have assumed kinship responsibilities.

The work of Leibow (1967), Ladner (1971), and Nobels (1975) describe the friendship/kinship system as it existed for Black males, adolescent females and families in major urban areas. Robert Staples (1978) summarizes the important role pseudokin played in the survival of the family.

The model of the Black family which has developed over time is one of an extended kinship system representing a number of distinct roles. This type of family structure also encompassed unreal kinsmen who assumed the rights and obligations of those related by genealogical bonds as a functional kinship grouping, it provided goods and services that individual families could not have obtained by their efforts alone. In the rural South the entire Black community would take on a primary character. As a group they maintained social control and regulated the behavior of individuals in accordance with their own moral code. (p. 77)

Stack (1974) explored the pseudokinship system of low income Blacks living in an urban housing development. She states that:

> The flexible expectations and extension of kin relationships to no-kin allow for the creation of domestic networks which are not bounded by genealogical distance or criteria. Much more important for the creation and recruitment to personal networks are the practical requirements that kin and friends live close together. (p. 61)

She found that the families, the majority of whom where living at a subsistence level, needed a steady source of cooperative support in order to survive. They were eager to share with one another because of the urgency of their needs. Friends and kin exchanged, gave and obligated one another. Being without such a flow of available goods could destroy a family's ability to survive.

The kinship patterns of middle class Black families has recently been studied by McAdoo (1979) and Barnes (1981). McAdoo interviewed 178 class families in Washington, D.C. and Columbia, Maryland. She found that the "Black Bourgeois" is not the disconnected or "uprooted" group of people sociologists once thought. These families have kept in close contact with their primary and extended kin groups; they give and receive substantial assistance in the form of money, care of children and talking out personal problems. She contends that the helping networks among Blacks are much more active than those of middle class Anglo, Catholic and Jewish immigrant families.

The Barnes (1981) study focused on the influence of socioeconomic factors on the interaction with kin, knowledge of genealogy, and knowledge of ante-bellum history. She conducted personal interviews with 41 couples residing in northeast Atlanta. Results revealed that kinship groups were still viable institutions kept alive by letter writing, telephone contact, personal contact, mutual help and ritual. Knowledge of kin was also strong among middle class families. However, the higher the social economic status the more likely Blacks would know only a few kinsmen.

A recent study by Dressler (1985) explored the relationship between social support and mental in southern Blacks. The influence of depression on a variety of social relationships was examined, including extended kin and perceived supportiveness of kin and non-kin. Conclusions indicated that people who perceive their extended kin to be more supportive report fewer symptoms of depression. The number of extended kin and perceived support of non-kin were unrelated to depression. A buffering effect of extended kin support on life events was evident in males. Extended kin support, however, was least effective in reducing the risk of depression among women.

In general, the results were consistent with Williams, et al. (1981), which finds social support to have a modest effect on psychological health. The author follows Thoits (1982) in stressing the importance of refining conceptual methodology on stress, support, and mental health. Dressler also suggests that further research focus on the role of the church and other social organizations that contribute to the healthy adjustment of Black community residents.

Thus, it appears that the major function of the primary/extended kinship system is to provide an atmosphere of emotional support, belonging, financial assistance, and to foster identity and self-worth. Billingsly (1968) uses the term "psychic security" to describe these functions.

This same sense of worth or belonging can also be found through contact with some formal and informal social institutions. The Black church has long been one such supportive institution. As previously stated, Hill (1972) found that strong religious orientation has been a key factor in the stability of Black families.

The present study attempted to examine the way in which individuals utilize their church social network in solving personal problems.The Black church in America was founded against a background of slavery and segregation and provided Blacks with the opportunity to be symbolically free while still in chains. According to Anderson (1982) Blacks have been found to be one of the most religious groups in America. This recent survey supports the work of Willie (1974) who contends that a strong religious orientation is found in many Black families regardless of their social class. Gibson (1983) found that Blacks were much more likely than whites to use prayer as a coping strategy, although this practice declined between 1957 and 1976.

Many writers have traced the historical origins of the Black church and its role and function in Black family life. Noted Black historian DuBois (1939) reports that the Black church is a center of social life. It acts as a newspaper and intelligence bureau by disseminating information, setting moral standards, promoting general intelligence and encouraging social betterment. Each church forms its own social circle and provides members with personal and spiritual support along with economic support. The church served as a comfortable way station for many Blacks migrating from the South. According to Myrdall (1944), "The chief function of the Negro church has been to buoy up the hopes of its members in the face of adversity and to give them a sense of community." (p. 83)

Ministers and elders of the Black church provide advice and counseling, as well as refer members to social service agencies. Hamilton (1972) states that although the minister continues to play an important role of counselor in the lives of many low income Blacks, it was his opinion that many upwardly mobile Blacks are moving out into other spheres of activity and are turning less to their preacher for help and more to mental health professionals for service.

Apart from the church and other formal social organizations such as the NAACP and the Masons, many non-traditional or informal institutions are found to be centers of social networks in the Black community. Liebow (1967) describes such an informal institution with a highly developed social network. " Tally's Corner" is a "major hang-out" for unemployed street corner men. The official structure is a small restaurant with a juke box, with Tally as the network's focal person. According to Liebow:

> The men who live in the area come together for effortless sociability. There is nothing to join, no one to say you belong. Some men are close friends, others consider themselves to be enemies. Each man mainly comes because others will be there. (p. 23)

The men of Tally's Corner comprise an extremely functional social network. Instrumental needs are met through assistance in "turning money" (finding work). The men meet each other's expressive needs by coming to each other's aid in crisis, providing guidance and psychological support.

Billingsly (1968) uses the tern "sub-society" to describe the other locations where such exchanges traditional occur. The laundromat, pool hall, barber shop, beauty shop, and tavern are examples of such community sub-societies. In this same vein, Bissonette (1977) studied how bartenders and hairdressers function as informal community gatekeepers who make social service referrals for people who are in emotional crisis. The author suggests that these community agents should be trained in crisis counseling since they act as a devised social network for many people.

SOCIAL NETWORKS AND HELP-SEEKING BEHAVIOR

Recently, social scientists have begun examining the way in which social networks influence attitudes and behavior. Particular attention is being given to the relationship between social networks, psychological adaptation and help-seeking behavior.

Tolsdorf (1976) attempts to look at the type of support that is most helpful during a crisis in his study of "Social Network Support and Coping." He focused attention on three specific functions of the social network: support, advice and feedback. Extensive interviews were conducted with ten recently hospitalized first admission psychiatric subjects and ten recently hospitalized medical subjects. All subjects were male and matched for marital status, education, and socioeconomic status. Data were collected on size and membership of social network, qualities of relationships, attitudes, beliefs, expectations of their network in helping them cope, and the nature of coping styles.

The psychiatric sample was found to have very limited social networks; they tended to receive more functions than they provided for others. They depended more on family and had fewer intimate relationships with others than the other medical sample. Their usage of social networks was termed "negative network orientation." They saw people in their network as lacking the expertise to help, giving only pity. Also, subjects did not want others to know of their problems or want to admit to having problems.

The medical sample was found to have a "positive network orientation"; they believed that the social network could be used for advice, support, and feedback during time of crisis. The medical sample also had more contact with and drew from a broader, stronger base of network resources.   In contrast, when the psychiatric subjects experienced some significant life stress, they attempted first to cope using individual mobilization or personal resources.   When this strategy failed, they chose not to mobilize their networks but relied instead only on themselves.

The work of Finlayson (1976) examined the relationship between social network orientation, psychological adaptation, and help-seeking behavior. Her study explored the coping resources of families where the husband had suffered a massive heart attack or had other serious heart disease. Data revealed that the husbands who had the most favorable outcomes were those with positive network orientation. In other words, those who accepted support and assistance from kin, friends, and the professional helping networks. In addition, some class differences were observed: the higher status families were the most inclined to use the non-kin network.

Hence, social networks appear to contribute to psychological adaptation and influence help-seeking behavior. In a recent review, Gourash (1978) lists four ways social networks influence help-seeking:

> 1) Buffering the experience of stress which obviates the need for help. 2) Precluding the necessity for professional assistance through a provision of instrumental and affective support. 3) Acting as screening and referable agents to professional services. 4) Transmitting attitudes, values, and norms about help seeking. (p. 416)

Other studies have investigated how help-seeking is affected by age, race, class, and education. Gurin, et al. (1960), found that help-seeking declined with age. Rosenblatt and Mayer (1972) found that professional help-seeking is more prevalent among white adults than Black.

Researchers have examined the importance of social class factors in influencing professional help-seeking and attitudes toward mental health. Rapheal (1964) found that social class was less important in predicting the use of psychiatric aid than the acceptance of this notion my one's community.   She used the term "compatible community culture" to describe the support given by the network to a person seeking professional help.

Hollingshead and Redlich (1965) concluded that people in the lower economic classes do not value and/or believe that psychiatric help can change their problems. The work of Kammeyer and Botton (1968) found that people were more likely to use services provided at a Family Service Center if the community understands and values their use. The class and level of education also influences their usage.

A recent (1978) study by Asser again explored the relationship between help-seeking and social classes as measured by occupation and education. The survey was conducted with 838 residents of Chicago and 42 extensive interviews were done. Special attention was paid to class, race, and age of the subjects. Respondents were classified as to whether they gave any evidence of valuing autonomy and self-direction or conformity to external authority and control. They were also rated as to whether their helping styles represented negotiating or didactic modes. Inferred in the didactic mode is the desire to have someone else take over the problem and find an immediate solution. The negotiating style involved recognition of one's role in the problem and the ability to conceptualize different solutions.

Findings indicated no evidence of an age or race effect. A sex by class effect was noted. The lower the social class, the more likely that males and females valued conformity and use of the didactic help-seeking behavior. The higher the female respondent's class the more likely she had used the negotiating help-seeking style. Males employed a didactic style regardless of class.

Lower class respondents appeared to be more influenced by the ideas and values of their social network than respondents from the higher class. Thus, they would encounter value conflicts with therapists who tend to be most often from middle-class income categories and, therefore, they would be more reluctant to seek help or drop out of therapy prematurely.

Fischer and Cohn (1972) found that help-seeking orientation was related to social class in their study of college students. They examined the relationship of help-seeking to educational level, religion, and academic major in a sample of 487 male and 502 female college students in Connecticut, New York City, and Washington, D.C. Data analyzed revealed differences in education level: juniors and seniors were more favorable to seeking professional help for psychological problems than underclassmen, and college freshmen were more positive than high school students. Jewish subjects tended to express more favorable attitudes than Catholics or Protestants in all economic classes. Social science majors were more favorable than students in other disciplines.

Since college students comprise a very atypical representation of subjects, it is difficult to generalize these findings to the population at large. However, Fischer and Cohn hypothesized that a social network system that includes people of different educational and social class levels would be more open to intervention from professional sources than a more closed and less educated network. But would those at the lowest end of the spectrum be influenced by those at the higher:

Many researchers have attempted to identify the ways in which social networks influence a person's decision to seek professional help, and the type that is sought. Kudushin (1969), McKinlay (1973), Kukla (1976), and Brown (1978) propose that help-seeking will vary according to the strength of personal resources and the type of help and suggestions that are offered by the social network, those whom McKinlay called "lay consultants."

McKinlay's study involved 87 working class families in Scotland and explored the apparent role of family, kin, and friendship networks in the utilization of services at a maternity clinic. Subjects were divided into two categories based on their utilization of services. "Utilizers" were women who attended clinic for ongoing prenatal care and post-delivery visits. "Underutilizers" were those who defaulted clinic appointments, attended for some form of care only after 28 weeks, or were admitted to treatment due to emergency.

Underutilizers were observed to be living in "a more crisis existence, dependent on relatives for housing and financial assistance. Husbands were chronically unemployed, and there was a great deal of marital instability." Utilizers, in contrast, lived more securely in independent housing with working husbands and wives and enjoyed stable marital arrangements. Results indicated that women who used health services had a more varied social network, and were able to make decisions independent of relatives and friends. Underutilizers relied more on the information of relatives and friends as lay consultants. Underutilizers were also found to have a higher frequency of contact with interlocking friendship/kinship system. Might one assume that peer pressure or opinions of their support system has a negative impact on their efforts to get professional service?

Horwitz (1977) followed the work of McKinlay in his study of social networks and psychiatric treatment. He proposed that people with strong supportive social networks would be less likely to seek psychiatric help; and that people with open and varied social networks will be more likely to seek psychiatric help. The sample consisted of 120 adults, outpatient and short-term inpatient clients. The results indicate that the structure of kin and friendship networks help shape the pathway to psychiatric treatment. Persons with strong support from kin but without open friendship networks were insulated from referrals and their kin were more tolerant of deviant behavior. Persons without strong kin networks but with open friendship systems received more network referrals, and entered treatment earlier with less severe problems.

Brown (1978) continued this notion in the investigation of 1,106 adults ages 20 to 70 years old residing in the Chicago area. His study focused on whether persons who sought help from informal lay consultants or formal professional sources were distinguishable from those who handled problems without assistance. Brown's results revealed a sharp drop in help-seeking, particularly informal contacts, among persons over 60 years of age. He suggests that older people should be the target for direct professional intervention, as well as programs designed to bolster their shrinking social network. Blacks appeared less likely to seek help than whites, especially Blacks with low income and education. The race difference was non-significant among more highly educated Black respondents. However, a recent (1983) study by Gibson appears to contradict this finding. Her study of elderly poor females found that Blacks in both middle and later life drew from a larger pool of informal helpers than white people. They were more versatile in substituting these helpers than white people. They were more versatile in substituting these helpers for one another as they advanced in age. Whites, in contrast, tended to rely more on spouses or a single family member as they grew older.

How people feel about asking and receiving help from others also has a definite impact on the utilization of services. The social norms constraining interpersonal help were studied by Schreiber and Glidewill (1978). They interviewed 348 middle and working class subjects who were also asked to specify their own rights and duties.

One of the most striking findings in the study was that only half of the respondents who received help form spouses, relatives, and friends believed they had a right to such help. Those respondents who felt they had a right to help from social networks showed three main patterns of reciprocity: emotional support, advice, and economic help. The respondents who felt they had a right to seek professional help appeared to feel more comfortable with receiving professional assistance because there was an exchange of money or direct payment.

Research has shown that people normally seek help from others with whom they are affiliated and in emergencies from strangers and professionals. Giving and receiving help from one's social network requires accepting inconvenience, extra trouble, and restricting individual desires.

Another important component to be examined in the under-utilization of psychological services is the process by which people decide to seek professional help. Kadushin (1969) brought insight to this subject and sought to identify factors influencing a person's decision to see a psychiatrist. 1,452 adults applying for treatment at 10 New York psychiatric centers were interviewed or mailed questionnaires, and their clinic records were examined. The sample population was primarily white protestant and East European Jews. According to Kadushin, the decision to consult a psychiatrist consists of four separate but related stages:

- realization of the problem;
- discussion of the problem with friends and relatives;
- choice of the type of professional healer to attend; and
- selection of a particular practitioner.

Kadushin found that the social network can exert influence as each major stage. The interpersonal relationships between family and friends can be the source of many emotional dilemmas and help problems to surface or develop. The people who are part of our social network help us to identify our problems or sources of conflict, and provide the necessary constraint or social control to limit harmful or inappropriate behavior.

Religion and social contacts also influence the selection of a practitioner and choice of treatment setting. Jewish respondents were found to be influenced by their religious training, and were more likely to attend a religiously affiliated treatment center. Kadushin used the term "friends and supporters of psychotherapy" to describe a group of well-educated, culturally sophisticated, upper income people who value and encourage the understanding of personality dynamics. This group actively suggested the names of clinicians and treatment facilities to others. Once in treatment, they remain for longer periods of time, and have a higher rate or return.

The Kadushin study also identified four categories of problems that are most often brought to professional counseling: physical symptoms, sexual problems, marital or primary group problems and major role problems. A class distinction was noted in that working class people tended to have complaints of physical symptoms; they most often were referred by physician, family, or employer, and primarily attended hospital clinics. The higher income clients complained more of sexual problems, marital conflicts and identity or role confusion.

More often they were self-referred and attended private or university-affiliated clinics.

Kukla, Veroff, and Douvan (1979) also identified a three-stage decision process in their study of social class and the use of professional help for personal problems. They are as follows:

1.   Defining the problem as a mental health problem (i.e., one relevant for professional help).

2.   Deciding to seek help.

3.   Selecting a particular source of help.

Their study examined the influence of socioeconomic status on each of the three stages. A sample of 2,464 adults were surveyed. The study replicated the work of Gurin (1960).

Results indicated that the relationship between family income and define a problem as relevant for help was not significant. However, higher educated people in both studies were more likely to define a problem in mental health terms, and actually seek help. Family income did appear to influence the choice of practitioner; low income families were more likely to seek the help of a clergyman. In terms of education, there is a greater use of psychologists and psychiatrists by the more educated subjects. The authors concluded that:

> The influence of education and income on help-seeking while holding constant reported levels of psychological distress, suggest that while distress plays a major role in seeking help, socioeconomic status differences in help-seeking behavior are largely independent of symptom levels. (p. 11)

Utilization studies indicate that children make up a large proportion of the population utilizing mental health services. Two authors, Lurie (1974) and Menaghan (1978) have attempted to identify factors that influence parents' decisions to seek professional psychological services for their children. Lurie's work was based on data derived from a study of emotional health of children in Westchester County, New

York. A stratified sample of 800 families was drawn, 20% Black. In the sample 15% were judged to be in clear need of help, and 13% were possibly in need of assistance; only 17% of those children in need of help at any time obtained psychiatric attention. The mothers were administered a questionnaire to help identify the concerns for their child's psychological health. The mothers were classified into two groups: worriers and non-worriers.

The findings included the fact that the portion of mothers that worried about their children rose with each socioeconomic level; also, more Jewish than non-Jewish mothers reported worrying about their children's behavior, and whites were more likely to worry than Blacks. Black mothers had twice as many children who were moderately to seriously disturbed than whites. Mothers who worried more often took the initiative to seek help for children with problems only after professional suggestion (i.e., doctor, teacher, or clergy). The kinds of services the children received reflected social class differences. Children from high income families obtained private care, primarily by psychiatrists and psychologists. Low income children received help from clinics, social agencies, and social workers. All parents utilized lay consultants before seeking professional help.

The Menaghan study specifically examined parents' concerns about their late adolescent and adult children. A sample of 551 adults was selected. Data revealed that the parental concern about children was strongest when the family was in the midst of change and the oldest child was between 21 and 25 years of age. The parents reporting the most concerns were more likely to be distressed and among those who sought help. Greater distress was associated with a limited use of family and other social network support, and a greater use of professional help.

In summary, the reviewed literature seems to suggest that social networks function to provide support to members during time of crisis and may be utilized by members as an alternative to seeking services at mental health facilities. Social networks have also been found to influence the individual's decision to seek professional help for personal problems in positive ways. The more educated and varied the social network and supportive the members are of psychotherapy, the more likely they are to encourage professional contact.

BLACKS' USE OF MENTAL HEALTH SERVICES

All the research cited indicates that Black people are less likely than whites to decide to seek professional help for psychological problems. According to Davis (1972) "Many Black people see going to mental health services as a ready admission of being crazy." Pierce (1972) contends that there are specific factors operating in the Black community that further influence the negative value attached to mental illness. The black community has a higher tolerance for chaotic or disruptive behavior because people have become conditioned to withstanding more environmental stress than whites. Thus, behavior that is considered disturbed or "crazy" would have to be of a more disruptive intensity in order to be viewed as outside the norm or abnormal. As a result, being mentally ill takes on a negative and threatening connotation associated with the crisis situation. (p. 399)

Cannon and Locke (1977) support his conclusion and state that Blacks as a group are probably more reluctant to admit a relative to a mental institution, especially a public facility, unless there is evidence of delusions, hallucinations or threat to harm oneself or others. This skepticism of the mental health system is apparently well-founded since Blacks historically receive more severe diagnoses, more medication, and are less often referred for long-term insight-oriented psychotherapy than whites. The inappropriate diagnosis of Black clients, along with subsequent long-term hospitalization at state facilities, has led community residents to view the mental health system as more oppressive than helpful.

McAdoo (1979) reports that there is a preference among middle class Black families to handle problems within the family system. These families do not perceive community social agencies as being particularly sensitive or helpful. As mentioned earlier, members of the extended Black family often function as counselors and advisors to others, as well as inhibitors when it comes to seeking professional service.

Similar findings are reported for Mexican Americans by Keefe (1978) and Padilla, Carlos and Keefe (1976). Mexican Americans tend to rely on non-professional sources for emotional support. Family, friends, and religious practitioners were most often used. Services at mental health centers were only sought in cases of severe disturbance (i.e., suicidal ideation or psychotic behavior).

Wolkon, Morwiceki and Williams (1973) examined the relationship of race, ethnicity and social class to attitudes toward help-seeking, race of therapist and self-disclosure. Findings indicate race alone was not related to attitudes toward psychotherapy, but social class was. However, Blacks from all income classes manifested lower self-disclosure scores than whites. Also, Blacks were more dissatisfied with treatment than whites and preferred a therapist of their own race.

Schneider, et al. (1980), examined the relations between perceptions of mental health providers and help-seeking. Their investigation involved Black, white, and Chicano community college students. Their findings conflict with the results reported by Wolkon, et al. They report that blacks and Chicanos are more likely than Anglos to take personal problems to a professional. The authors offer two explanations for this unusual trend. The first is that Anglos may have a different (actually lower) likelihood of seeking help from providers because they have been familiar with mental health professionals long enough to know that counseling can hurt as well as help. A second explanation is that minorities experience more difficulties and are more concerned about their difficulties and thus seek professional help. It could also be hypothesized that the students would be more open to seeking professional help because of their level of education and exposure to people who support such behavior.

Dawkins, Terry and Dawkins (1980) studied the differences between users and non-users of mental health services. A sample of 60 Black adult inner city residents was administered personality and lifestyle inventories. Users were found to be more dependent, unmotivated, and socially withdrawn, while non-users showed more tendency towards social deviancy. Both groups scored relatively high on neurotic and psychopathic measures of defensiveness, psychic pain, impulsiveness, and potential for psychotic reactions.

These findings seem to indicate that inner city residents experience more psychic distress which makes them more susceptible to developing emotional problems and that they enter the mental health system with more serious problems. These conclusions support the work of Pierce (1972).

In summary, the reported literature indicates that Blacks are skeptical of seeking professional mental health services, and that they prefer to discuss issues within their primary social network. Being part of a closed network system would greatly reduce the likelihood of their receiving support for the decision to seek professional help unless their network members also valued this experience. Moreover, the body of literature reviewed seems to indicate that patterns of help-seeking or utilization of services are influenced by education, race, social class, family, social networks, and our own attitudes about giving and receiving help, which are affected by these same influencing factors.

Community mental health centers will probably continue to under-serve black clients until they have more knowledge of where people go to receive help and who they feel most comfortable with. Knowledge of social networks could have many implications for community mental health policy and practice. Intervention strategies should focus on the individual as well as the community. According to Mayfield (1972) mental health programs must focus energies on changing the adverse conditions that exist in the Black community. This would seem to be more productive for achieving the long-range goals of community mental health programs than if their major efforts focused on helping Black patients adjust to these conditions. (p. 118)

Solomon (1976) adds that:

> The key to positive evaluation of mental health services in black communities may well be the extent to which these services successfully counter-act the myth of negative evaluation and reduce feelings of powerfulness for black clients. To achieve this goal, consummate attention must be

given to engaging the client in a problem-solving
effort. (p. 315)

Mental health professionals who wish to assist Black clients in
changing their life situations need to have an understanding of
community dynamics and institutions that link the community to the
people. Knowing these networks and their functions will be beneficial to the development of appropriate prevention projects which help
reduce the incidence of mental illness through early identification of
problems, and consultation and education services. The work of
Taber (1972) and Brooks (1974) are examples of two such programs.
Taber describes how a social club, "The Noble Teens" helped to
improve peer relationships with a group of identified clients while
also helping to reduce gang violence in the neighborhood. Brooks
organized a cooperative mothers' group and a family night activity to
assist people having difficulty with parent/child conflicts. Social
network therapy can also be effectively used in family intervention
with extended or multi-generation families.

Social networks provide guidance, encouragement, and financial
assistance during times of crises (Billingsly, 1968; Turkat, 1980).
Clinical studies indicate the absence of social supports is associated
with increased psychological distress (Tolsdorf, 1976; Turner, 1979),
which seems to infer a relationship between social support and well-
being (Andrews, et al., 1978; Linn, et all., 1979).

Research also reports a relationship between social networks and use
of medical and psychological services (Fischer and Cohn, 1972;
McKinlay, 1973; Finlayson, 1976). Those people with networks who
are knowledgeable of psychotherapy and are supportive of its use are
more likely to seek services (Kadushin, 1969). The work of McKinlay
(1973); Fischer and Cohn (1972); and Finlayson (1976); also indicate
that people with varied networks and those composed of family
friends and other social contacts were more open to professional
intervention.

The present study attempted to provide descriptive information on
the role and function of social networks in the lives of Blacks in
prison and also the impact of social networks on help-seeking

behavior. The following hypotheses incorporated the aforementioned research in the examination of the relationships of social network support with social well-being and professional help-seeking for psychological problems. Following the suggestion of Leavy (1983) and Dressler (1985), information was gathered to ascertain the relationship between social network satisfaction, perceived support, and network utilization during times of emotional stress.

Hypotheses

1. There is a positive association between social network satisfaction and social well-being.

2. Social network satisfaction will be associated with network utilization for emotional problem-seeking behavior.

3. There is a positive association between social well-being and network utilization for emotional problems.

The results of the study contribute to the development of treatment models that are sensitive to the unique culture of Blacks in prison and in America. Additionally, the results provide information for the prison and the larger community gatekeepers who can help identify individuals who are in need of psychological help at the onset of the problem. They also identify individuals and social institutions that can be utilized in the creation of primary prevention programs.

CHAPTER THREE

RESEARCH METHODOLOGY FOR THE STUDY AND UNDERSTANDING OF SOCIAL NETWORK SYSTEMS AMONG BLACK ADULT PRISON OFFENDERS

RESEARCH METHODOLOGY

The three factors examined were social network satisfaction, social well-being, and help received for emotional problems in a representative sample of Black adults. The present research employs a correlational design, because the variables examined are complex and do not lend themselves to controlled manipulation. This design allowed for the explanation of the extent to which variations in one factor correspond with variations in other factors. The two major advantages of this approach are the ability to measure several variables and their interrelationships simultaneously, and the ability to measure degrees of relationship. (Issac and Michael, 1971).

DATA COLLECTION

A questionnaire designed to measure social network satisfaction, social well-being, and help-seeking was administered to resident offenders of "Lakeside Prison." This is a desegregated prison where Blacks comprise 52% of the population. "Lakeside Prison" is located in a small midwestern town (population 39,000). There are several small factories and two major steel manufacturers located in surrounding cities which employ the majority of the "Lakeside Prison" residents, but "Lakeside Prison" has been the stable source of employment for a large segment of this community.

The social life of the prison is organized within the contexts of the bureaucratic structure (superintendent, assistant superintendents, professional and custody staff and offenders who are in the majority and mostly Black. The Lakeside Prison, under court order, has provided improved social, medical, educational and psychological services for its offenders populations.

PROCEDURE

The first phase of the research involved collecting demographic information using the prison classification system. The second phase of the research was a survey of offenders in the residential prison to gather information on social network supports, group participation, social network satisfaction, social well-being, and help-seeking for psychological problems. Each residential offender was contacted and given an opportunity to participate in the project during the Phase I process.

A total of 110 offenders were selected. The interviews sample of 57 constituted a response rate of 60.59%. Non-response was moderate. Non-respondents were divided between refusals and non-contacts. Potential respondents were dropped if they could not be reached after two attempts.

All interviews were conducted by the investigator during one session. The length of the interview session varied between 15 minutes and an hour. The signed consent form was obtained at the beginning of the interview. Demographic information was gathered first, followed by a brief support-building exercise. The offender-respondent was able to ask clarification on questions and was also allowed to review the written response on their questionnaire. Responses were recorded verbatim.

SUBJECTS - OFFENDERS

A total of 110 adult offenders were surveyed for the study. Forty-four did not complete the questionnaires and they were eliminated from the original sample. 98% of these individuals were white offenders. Many of them claimed privately that past surveys of this nature have not reported any benefits for them and since it was not mandatory, they refused to return the questionnaires or to provide further information for lack of participation. Thus, though not intended, this study was able to obtain little over half of its question-naires from the Black offenders. This may have been a blessing in disguise since we know little or nothing as to how offenders, and in particular, Black offenders engage in imprisoned social network system.

The demographic characteristics of the population samples are as follow:

VARIABLE   **% + OF TOTAL**

1. AGE

A.	18 or under	1.8%
B.	19-25	5.4%
C.	26-35	37.5%
D.	36-45	33.9%
E.	46 or over	21.4%

2. NATURE OF OFFENSE

A.	Class A	62.1%
B.	Class B	29.35%
C.	Class C	8.6%

3. MARITAL STATUS

A.	Single	32.1%
B.	Married	39.3%
C.	Separated	7.2%
D.	Divorced	19.6%
E.	Widowed	1.8%

4. ETHNIC GROUP

A.	Black-American	56.9%
B.	Oriental	-----
C.	Spanish-Speaking	-----
D.	White-American	39.7%
E.	Native-American	3.4%

5. SIZE OF COMMUNITY LIVED IN BEFORE INCARCERA-
   TION

A.	Farm			1.7%
B.	Village	250-2,499	Population	-----
C.	Town	2,500-24,999	"	16.1%
D.	City	25,000-99,999	"	30.45%
E.	City	Over 100,000	"	51.8%

CHAPTER FOUR

BLACK OFFENDERS' NETWORK SYSTEM TOWARD MEETING THEIR SOCIAL AND PSYCHOLOGICAL NEEDS

With regard to the prison offenders' social network system, there were several questions asked as to what extent offenders receive help in spite of the former psychological system. We know from social science studies that people seek advice and help from friends and relatives other than professionals who are supposed to be ones to assist in areas of meeting their social-psychological needs.

Our finding shows, indeed, offenders have turned and will continue to turn to friends and family when confronted with serious social/psychological problems.

For example, on Table 1 the question: "About how often were you on the telephone with close friends or relatives during the past month?" The results are as follows:

a.	Every day	7.7%
b.	Several times a week	12.3%
c.	About once a week	38.5%
d.	2 or 3 times a week	29.2%
e.	Not at all	12.3%

As clearly shown, 38% of residential offenders stated they telephone close friends or relatives about once a week; 29% said they make calls 2 or 3 times a week. 12% of this survey population claim they do not call at all. This indicates that the overwhelming majority of the population is in contact with close friends as significant persons they can count on in time of trouble.

The pervasive telephone calling also supports the notion that the residential offender group does have a so-called "out reach" social network system that is supportive of them and keeps family and friendship ties closely knitted to meet social, economical, and psychological needs.

To determine to what extent our offender populations is faring with others as part of the social network system, we asked: "In general, how well are you getting along with other people these days?"

Table 2

a.	Better than usual	26.8%
b.	About the same	71.45%
c.	Not as well as usual	1.85%

As indicated above, 26.8% said better than usual and 71% stated about the same. In short, the vast majority feel they are getting along with other people pretty well. Perhaps, the reason for these good reported interpersonal relations is based upon having access to telephones to call and talk with friends and family, as well as friends among their own peers. Telephone calls are a part of a social network system which appears to be working among the surveyed group.

We wanted to know to what extent religious services played a part in the offender's social network system. It has been suggested by some psychologists that meeting spiritual needs is as relevant to psychological well-being as other social needs. We are not assuming religious services are the only way to meet spiritual needs, but religious services in a prison residential setting are most accessible to the offenders toward meeting that particular need. We asked the question: "How often have you attended a religious service during the past month?"

Table 3

a.	Every day	1.8%
b.	More than once a week	8.9%
c.	2 or 3 times in past month	8.9%
d.	Once in past month	10.75%
e.	Not at all in past month	69.6%

The vast majority of the residential offenders surveyed have not attended religious services in the past month.

It should be stated that we have not had religious services on a regular basis within this dormitory setting. One reason is that we just recently employed a Protestant Chaplain. Most of the residents are Protestant. However, the main reason for such low participation in religious services may be attributed to minimum religious training prior to their conviction and lack of social networking within the religious community to attack persons with criminal backgrounds.

Also, the authoritarian attitudes are portrayed by many official members of the religious community. Be that as it may, it appears that the network toward meeting spiritual needs is not present in the religious services program with these residential offenders.

We are also concerned about offenders' participation in other group activities which fostered social network behavior. We asked them: "What kind of volunteer groups or organizations do you belong to or attend?"

Table 4

1.	Jaycees Organization	10.0%
2.	Lifers Club	25.0%
3.	Recreational Activities	12.1%
4.	Basketball League	12.2%
5.	Softball League	15.0%
6.	AMVETS	5.0%
7.	A.A.	3.0%
8.	Religious Services	18.7%

Since most of the offenders are under a life sentence, it would be almost obvious that a large number of them would belong to a Lifers Club. 25% of our residential offenders reported being a member of this organization. However, the vast majority reported participation in recreational and athletic activities with religious services being the second highest area of group participation-18%. This also supports the notion that offenders develop social network behavior in other social areas such as recreational/athletic activities that may bring some satisfaction into their lives in helping them to meet non-aggressive as well as aggressive needs in an acceptable manner.

Do the activities mentioned above lead toward future goal-planning for future network behavior among these offenders? The projected question is: "As you consider your future goals in life, which of the following is most important to you?"

Table 5

a.	Obtaining a reasonably high status in community		9.9%
b.	Being able to help other people		32.1%
c.	Achieving a certain amount of power in the community		34.65%
d.	Accumulating a sufficient amount of money to be able to live well		15.95%
e.	Helping to make the society a better place for people to live		23.4%

It is interesting to note that the future goals of a vast majority of the offenders in this survey are to help others, to achieve a certain amount of power and to make the society a better place for people to live.

If we tie all three of these goals together, we are talking about "people power." This notion suggests networking to make it work for the betterment of our society. However, the future goals of about 25% of offenders surveyed are acquiring a high stature and sufficient amounts of money to live well in a community setting.

In addition to these offenders networking with "in-house" activities, as discussed, we wanted to understand to what extent outside contacts with families and friends influenced behavior, as well as what support offenders receive in time of crisis and from whom, so we asked the following question: "Do you receive help/support from your friends when you are having personal problems/feeling emotionally upset?"

Table 6

A lot of help	33.9%
Some help	33.9%
Little help	68.0%
No help at all	0%
Don't ask for help	25.4%

Little over 60% of these offenders reported receiving a lot of help and some help from their friends when they are having personal problems. However, on the other hand, 25% said they did not ask for help when they were having problems or feeling emotionally upset.

We asked on Table 7: "Are you satisfied with help you receive?" 91.4% stated they were very satisfied to just being satisfied. 8.6% were dissatisfied, to very dissatisfied. The latter percent (8.6) accounts for the group that stated earlier they did not ask for help. Also part of it might be that the people they were asked were unable to suggest alternatives toward solution to their problems or conflicts.

We were interested in knowing who our offender population would turn to for help within a dormitory setting. On Table 8 we asked them the following question: "If you were having emotional problems, which one of the following professionals would you seek for help? You may check more than one answer."

1.	Psychiatrist	16.9%
2.	Psychologist	23.0%
3.	Unit Team Members	14.5%
4.	Counselor	13.6%
5.	Correction Officer	7.6%
6.	Mental Health Center	1.7%
7.	Hospital	1.7%
8.	Other	76.9%
9.	None	0.95%

For some unknown reason, the 23% of offenders in this particular survey see the psychologist as the person they are most likely to turn to when having emotional problems. The psychiatrist with 16% was the second professional they would seek out for help.   36% of offenders combined would seek help from the counselor, unit team members, correction officer, etc.   5.1% of the offenders would not seek any help from the above list of helpers.

It appears we are attempting to manage one-third of the offenders who have considerable mistrust for certain professional staff members.   It would be wise for these staff members to develop a communication system with these offenders in an attempt to earn their trust and respect.

Since we found out who these offenders would turn to with their emotional problems, we also wanted to know what types of emotional problems they were experiencing. We asked the following question: "Are you having emotional problems with any of the following?" The results are presented in Table 9

Table 9

1.	Problem with staff	20.5%
2.	Problem with job placement	12.8%
3.	Problem with other offender	2.6%
4.	Problem with spouse-girlfriend	5.1%
5.	Problem coping with divorce, death of person	
		5.1%
6.	Feeling depressed	17.9%
7.	Feeling anxious	5.1%
8.	Other	30.8%

31% of our offender population said they were having emotional problems with "other" problems than the ones mentioned. Perhaps we made a mistake by leaving an open ended question because we do not know what the "other" was. However, 20.5% stated they are having emotional problems with staff. 17% feel depressed; 12% are having problems with job assignment and over 10% intraemotional problems.

The K-Dormitory staff have, since this questionnaire was administered, "treated" a great number of these problems. For example, this writer has provided psychological services & referred individual offenders for their depressive states. Many of our residents are just now "learning states" in which they must find means and ways of getting along with their job foreman, as well as members of the immediate K-Dormitory staff members. This was a hard lesson for some, because supervision and responsibility have been things of their lost past.

We also wanted to know if those who were experiencing emotional problems and seek help form health professionals would get support from their peers. On Table 10, 86% reported that their peers would be very supportive to supportive. Only 7.1% said their friends would be nonsupportive. The majority (67%) of residential offenders do not see their friends having much influence and most think the most influential factor in a person's decision to seek help is realizing, or knowing that they have a problem and being able to discuss the problem with a friend or relative.

In order to meet the psychological service needs of this multi-racial cultural group of offenders, we asked the following question: On Table 11: "Which of the following psychological services best fit your present needs?"

Personal Counseling	20.0%
Group Psychotherapy	10.9%
Stress Management	5.5%
Career Education	30.95
Drug-Substance Abuse	3.6%
Interpersonal Relations	1.8%
Value Clarification	0%
Human Relations Group	9.1%
Marital-Family Counseling	9.1%
Individual Psychotherapy	3.3%
Others	5.5%

30.9% of the offenders studied said career education. 10% stated personal counseling best fists their present need. Only 10% saw group psychotherapy as a present need or interest.

It is suspected that because most of these offenders are close to community reintegration, career education in terms of job placement

is their number one objective. With regards to what the offenders
see as the greatest mental health problems interfering with their
development as persons since being on medium release, the following
Table 12 indicates their feeling:

Table 12

1.	Employment assignment	9.6%
2.	Housing arrangement	7.0%
3.	Adjusting to being on trusty status	1.8%
4.	Interpersonal relations	4.4%
5.	Staff-offender relations	8.8%
6.	Hygiene-personal/environmental	5.3%
7.	Food services	11.4%
8.	Medical services	7.9%
9.	Psychological services	2.6%
10.	Religious services	4.4%
11.	Race relations	11.4%
12.	Recreational services	2.6%
13.	Social service (visits, accounts, counseling)	
		7.7%
14.	None of the above	15.8%

A small minority of the offenders, 15.8% surveyed did not see any of
the above issues interfering with their growth and development being
residential setting. However, the majority of the group found at least
one issue interfering with their residential adjustments. It appears
that employment, food and race relations caused some amount of
institutional unrest. 9%, 11%, and 12%, respectively, see employment, assignment, food and race relation as the greatest mental
health problem interfering with their development since being
assigned to K-Dormitory. However, 49% of the offenders surveyed
said that they were satisfied with job opportunities at K-Dormitory
and 51% reported being satisfied with the living arrangement.

IMPLICATION FOR PRACTICE AND RESEARCH

After initial analysis is completed, the logical question remains: What do residents of K-Dormitory Prison Residential Community want for themselves?

The offenders see race relation and job assignment as present issues for the institution to do something toward remedying the situation. A large number of offenders see a need for career education and personal counseling, which seem to have quite a bit of importance attached to them.

In the field of mental health, the offenders seem to want a reexamination of the entire helping relations process. That process that affects their health is seen as crucial to future success, hence, the process itself must adapt itself to needs. Quality psychological service is to be achieved through the inclusion of more sensitive personnel to the psychological program in the prison environment where policy is made. Perhaps more self-awareness programs are needed.

As we said earlier, this pilot study falls under the category of social linkage and is concerned with the by-product of the social interaction relative to meeting offender's needs.

It appears from this brief study that offenders' needs are being met more from an outreach social network system than from within the residential environment. There are many reasons for this finding. As discussed earlier, the social network of family and kin group suggest mutual responsibility, caring concerns, and strong mutual identification, which is rightly so. Staff cannot and should not serve as a substitute for individuals meeting these needs. We should, however, strengthen our ties with offenders so that it is possible to share in their social network system. We, too, should be a part of the social linkage. Being a social barrier toward better understanding leading to reintegration for all should be a goal of our program.

PRISON RESIDENTIAL DORMITORY

Wherever it may fit in the spectrum of the correctional services, the Prison dormitory should provide a programmed and supervised transition to productive community living for selected offenders. The programs should be as flexible as possible, geared specifically to management needs and directed toward each resident achieving progressive self-sufficiency in later community setting.

From the varied limited pilot research, experience and observation of the prison residential dormitory, a number of basic principles and operating guidelines have emerged. The following are the greatest importance:

> 1. A residential dormitory can hope to function effectively only as far as they have ready access to the prison community resources needed for programs support, job opportunities, programs of education and training, clinical and professional services and general prison acceptance.
>
> 2. Responsibility for decision-making with respect to admissions and removals of residents should be vested in the K-Dorm Unit 8 Treatment Team. This will require the closest possible collaboration with correctional administrators, who share responsibility for the proper and effective use of the dormitory.
>
> 3. Assessment of the needs of offenders served by the dormitory should receive early consideration. There must be general agreement by those concerned that (a) substantial need exists and (b) a significant number of these can be met by an adequate residential dormitory program.
>
> 4. In all areas of internal programs, emphasis should be given to each resident's involvement in his own plan. He must be motivated to develop it and carry it through. Staff involvement should be

limited to guidance, clarification and identification of alternatives. Staff should concentrate on strategies for thrusting the residents into increasingly demanding situations approximating those he will encounter when he is on his own when there will be a few controls and limited support.

5. Dormitory staff should initiate a process of situation-oriented counseling for each resident. Focused on day-to-day performance and adjustment difficulties encountered, this type of counseling clarifies three points:

1. Prospective problems experienced by the resident

2. Suggest appropriate choices for dealing with them

3. Provide some control over impulsive reactions to the stresses and frustrations which occur.

THE FUTURE OF PRISON-BASED PROGRAMS

That the number and kinds of correctional programs in the prison community will continue to multiply, and that programs' staff will continually strive to improve operational efficiency, is beyond question. Increasing the correctional benefits of such programs is a more complex problem.

It is certain that the prison-based programs with or without other program innovations will solve but a few of the many problems besetting the prison. Long-range planning and coordinated efforts will be needed, together with the kinds of resources which will produce better understanding of the entire correctional prison process and enable close study of whatever steps are taken to improve the system.

In closing, my clinical impression is that psychological service for offenders in K-Dormitory Residential setting, as alluded to in this manuscript, has been beneficial to some degree for the majority of those who were contacted. Among the benefits were: (1) an ability to discuss their problems, (2) new information, (3) self-awareness, 4) assumption of responsibility for their action, (5) alteration in goals, values and life styles. Although the work is difficult and demanding, the results offset the hardship of the task.

CHAPTER FIVE

THE BLACK OFFENDER AND THE
SOCIAL NETWORK SYSTEM

The intended purpose of this chapter based on the findings of this study is to assist the individual who chooses to work with Blacks and Non-Whites and poor offenders in prison systems and in the formulation of a coherent approach to treatment, intervention, and reintegration. Universal awareness of the problems caused by the failure of the nation's prisons to meet their biosociological-psychological needs is growing. Broad measures of their presence are seen in the reported "behind the walls" criminal activities, as well as escalating drug and sex abuse, indicating a necessity to develop more community-based correctional facilities for both rural and urban offenders who, while a minority of the overall population, represent a majority of those who are incarcerated.

The profile of these offenders will be briefly mentioned here and defined more clearly in the text that follows.

A number of theories attempt to explain how people become professional criminals: poverty causes crime, "bad" neighborhoods cause crime: movies, television, comic books and radio crime stories cause crime; criminal associates cause crime; broken homes cause crime; race, nationality, sex neuroses, or crowded housing causes crime. These theories or notions do not explain why most poor people, particularly poor Black people, never become professional criminals. Nor do most people from "bad" neighborhoods, or most children from single parent or broken homes, or most of any race or sex, or most neurotics become criminals. If crowded housing caused crime, practically all Navajos (Native Americans) would be criminals; but actually, very few would be classified as such.

There is a difference between a professional criminal and a prison offender. The latter is an occasional lawbreaker, drug abuser, or alcoholic or person who murders or steals in a passionate outbreak. Our jails are filled with these amateur or so-called neurotic offenders who play cops and robbers, who get a kick out of tearing up a place or doing something they feel will not get them caught. The person who becomes a professional criminal, however, usually does so because he believes that he is expected to be a "Boragtist", an outlaw, by those he takes seriously: his parents, friends, neighbors, teachers, clergymen, police, social workers, or judges. He comes to view himself as different, as requiring a vocation different from those around him; and he begins to identify--and associate--with persons who have been ostracized like himself. Both the offender and the professional come in contact with the criminal justice system; however, it is the professional criminal that is less likely to be detected and serve time in a correctional facility.

We are concerned in treatment with both the criminal and the offender, and we are particularly concerned in this discussion with Blacks. Simply because there is less reported emphasis placed on treatment programs geared for Black offenders toward their reintegration process, they tend to be in the jails and repeat serious crimes in numbers out of proportion with their national census. Additionally, for those individuals reared in the before-mentioned environment, there is a higher incidence of engaging in illegal behavior as defined by the larger community. This notion will be further elaborated on later in our discussion.

Blacks in America have a higher probability than Whites of having involvement with the police; and once having made contact, they have a greater likelihood of being arrested, of being arraigned, of being convicted, and of being sent to prison. This accounts, in part, for the substantial number of Blacks--as mentioned earlier, well out of proportion to their representation in the nation's population--who are clients in the Criminal Justice System. Conversely, staffs of these institutions contain fewer Blacks proportionately. Bitterness, resentment, and a feeling among Black offenders that prison is a continuance of the White man's social discrimination, are not unusual. It appears that the situation is the same for Chicanos, Native Americans, Puerto Ricans, and all poor people.

Have mental health professionals and behavioral scientists participated in public policy decisions which will alter this imbalance? Will they be able to influence social, economic, and political forces to

help change this state of being? Can the behavioral sciences find
methods for providing opportunities for Blacks and other Non-White
groups to achieve their goals through legitimate means, increase their
commitment to conventional activities, build generalized bonds with
society, and promote a sufficient level of satisfaction so that many of
the social problems will no longer exist? These are the demanding
tasks; and they demand immediate action. We can no longer afford
to wait, exacerbating the problems and prolonging the arrival at
ultimate solutions. No longer can we rationalize our lack of progress
by saying we are waiting until other disciplines are prepared to
moved forward with us.

Later in this book some tentative therapeutic programs that have
worked with Blacks and are leading them toward self-realization will
be suggested. These programs might provide the corner stone of a
prison policy toward promoting the reintegration process.

With the increase of Black offenders in penal institutions, many
prison therapeutic staffs will be working with Black offenders for the
first time. Still other prison personnel without understanding of the
Black experience have been working with Black offenders in a
"handicapping"--rather than a "helping"--way.   The fundamental
question is, "Can prison staff effectively deal with the social problems
affecting the reintegration of Black offenders in prison systems?" The
contention of this writer is that education training programs have not
adequately prepared prison staff for this crossover role.   This is
because of class and racial differences of Black offender regards
many prison staff personnel as the "enemy." In addition, there are
certain cultural barriers, such as ignorance of the Black offender's
background, language, and other preconceived racial attitudes, that
interfere with effective treatment processes directed at the Black
offender.   We feel this problem is further compounded by the
problems of social class differences between the Non-Black therapist
and the Black offender in the prison system.

We have suggested and argue for the training of paraprofessionals
and indigenous counselors. We question whether training White
therapists will make them more sensitive to Black offenders. One of
the problems here is that in very few instances has such training been
attempted. Many members of prison staffs will continue to handicap

Black self-realization and growth patterns unless they receive some sort of intensive training from the Black perspective. Traditional higher education in therapeutic service programs typically are geared strictly toward preparing the student therapist for working with people who will enter or reenter the cultural mainstream.

It is believed by this writer that the staff therapist must be bicultural. He must not only have internalized mainstream culture, but must have been exposed extensively to Black culture as well. He must not impose mainstream norms on Black offenders. In order for trust to develop in the relationship, it is vitally important that the staff therapist be able to relate to Black culture in an objective rather than subjective fashion. It is not highly recommended that the staff therapist alienate his "whiteness" or present himself as a Black man or woman by using slang, Black handshakes, etc., but he must have a genuine understanding of the Black experience. The Black client will be turned off to a person who tries to come too close, too soon. The staff therapist should be certified by Black and White therapists as having met basic training requirements for dealing with Blacks.

DIFFERENCE AND DEFICIT MODEL ORIENTATION

The therapist must reject the model which states that Blacks have a weakness or deficiency based solely on genetic and environment factors. He must employ the differences between Black and White life styles, noting that they are not the result of pathology, deficiencies, faulty learning, or genetic inferiority (Williams, 1971). These differences are clearly manifestations of a viable Black American culture which probably is necessary for purposes of survival.

"NEGRO" AND BLACK

To be a Black man in contemporary America has certain connotations regarding self definition. The Black man sees education as a vehicle for social change; he believes group goals are more important than individual goals; he selects leaders based on competence, not status; he is pro-Black, not necessarily anti-White; he sets norms and defines goals in terms of self-determination; there is a sense of urgency about his goals.

It is also important for the prison therapist to realize that all Black offenders do not have so-called "negative self images", or the "self-hatred" phenomena so often ascribed to Blacks. Black offenders--like the majority of Black people in America--have pride, high self regard, and a feeling of self worth and importance. Black skin, kinky hair, flat noses and thick lips are considered unique, not ugly parts of the Black body image. The "Negro", however, has many "hang-ups" about his self concepts because his self definitions are based on White standards.

The Black offender's burdens, mental problems, hopes, dreams, and aspirations differ greatly from other Americans. When a people is segregated by force or by choice, different orientations, norms, and expectations develop. American society, namely Non-Black Americans, has not paid sufficient attention to understand the Black psyche or Black lifestyles. Too much emphasis has been placed on understanding similarities and differences between Blacks and Non-Blacks. Comparative research should be prohibited as it has no scientific rationale anyway. Comparative research is basically a spin-off from the racist ideology, accomplishing nothing worthwhile.

The prison staff must not take the attitude that they are dealing with another offender. We must realize that we are dealing with, in most cases, a Black offender, who hurts because of the "system" and not because of Oedipal conflicts. If the staff person is racist or has any misunderstanding of the Black experience, he should not be permitted to work with Black offenders. If the staff person cannot make a commitment, he must not engage a Black offender in a counseling relationship.

Some mental health researchers and scholars have become increasingly aware of the cultural biases in the therapeutic environment. In particular, the feeling has been growing among Black and Non-Black behavioral scientists that psychotherapy and counseling, rooted mainly in European culture as it was and is today, is not relevant to many contemporary Americans with mental health problems. This may be especially true for those social groups on the edge--or even further out--of the mainstream of American culture: certain racial or ethnic groups, those who live in poverty, or those with other specific--and separating--concerns, like Black offenders in our prison systems.

"The Challenge of Crime in a Free Society", a report by the President's Commission on Law Enforcement and Administration of justice, presented the first accurate picture--nationally--of the number of offenders under correctional authority on an average day: 1.3 million.   This total is so much larger than had ever before been estimated that it has startled even those most familiar with the field. It indicates a serious overtaxing of the facilities, programs, and personnel of the correctional system. Moreover, if present trends in arrests and convictions continue, the system will be facing even more pressures. The juvenile system, because of the rapid increase in the number of young people in the population, will be the most hard-pressed.   Adult probation and parole treatment will also suffer, because of the trend toward probation or early parole rather than prolonged confinement. In recent years, adult institutional commitments have been leveling off.

The document further presents general characteristics of the offenders, but not by racial breakdown. However, it was reported in viewpoint #5 on minorities and prisons that minorities are in correctional institutions out of proportion to their numbers. One-third of all offenders are Black, but they represent only one-tenth of the total population. The President's Commission on Law Enforcement and Administration of Justice explained that:

> Offenders themselves differ strikingly. Some are irrevocably committed to criminal careers; others subscribe to quite conventional values; still others, probably the majority, are aimless and frustrated youths.   Many others are alcoholics, narcotics addicts, victims of senility, and sex deviates. This diversity poses immense problems for correctional officials, for in most places the many special offender groups must be managed within large, general purpose programs.   The superintendent of an institution must meet the challenge of especially hostile and violent inmates, respond appropriately to

those who are mentally disordered, guard against the smuggling and use of narcotics, provide instruction and supervision for the mentally retarded, and handle the dangerous and intricate problem of sexual deviance, all within a locked and artificial world.

Beneath the diversities, certain characteristics predominate. A great majority of offenders are male. Most of them are young: in the age range between 16 and 30. The life histories of most of them document the way in which the social and economic factors contribute to crime and delinquency. Education is as good a barometer as any of the likelihood of success in modern urban society; a high proportion of offenders are severely handicapped educationally. Many of them have dropped out of school.

Offenders also tend to have unstable work records and a lack of vocational skills. A large proportion come from groups that suffer economic and social disadvantage and backgrounds of poverty. Material failure, then, in a culture firmly oriented toward material success, is the most common denominator of offenders. Some have been automatically excluded from economic and social opportunity; some simply have not tried hard enough. Many, too, have failed in their relationships with their families and friends. Offenders, adult and juvenile, usually have little self-esteem and for some it is only when they are undergoing correction that they get a first glimmer of the personal worth.

REINTEGRATION OF BLACK OFFENDERS

Among Black offenders recidivism is a major social problem in the urban community today. Most of the persons arrested for serious crime have been arrested before. Indeed, one recent study estimates that over 87% of those arrested will have been previously arrested; or, put a bit differently, the probability of being rearrested is .87 chances in one, or close to certainly. Other studies have shown that the chance of being rearrested are at least 70%. The rearrest rates suggest that for recidivists the arrest itself is little or no deterrent. One in every three offenders is a recidivist and it is these recidivists who commit the most serious crimes. Evidently, many penal and correctional institutions are not having positive results with their reintegration programs. For a great many offenders, corrections do not correct. Indeed, experts are increasingly coming to think that the conditions under which many offenders are handled, particularly in institutions, are often a positive detriment to reintegration. However, the rate of recidivism can be reduced with a good program aimed toward reintegrating offenders. This has been proven in other countries.

The price we pay for crime, both as victims and as taxpayers, is far greater than an intelligent pre-and post-reintegration program would cost. Peter Garwood, author of "To Catch a Career Criminal" (Newsweek, 1982), after interviewing 2,190 offenders, has isolated seven characteristics that he stated could be used to predict a high rate of criminal activity:

* imprisonment for more than two years preceding the most recent arrest;

* a previous conviction for the same crime;

* a conviction before the age of sixteen;

* commitment to a juvenile facility;

* heroin or barbiturate use in the preceding two years;

* use of the same drugs as a juvenile; and

* unemployment for more than half of the preceding two years.

Recidivists usually spend their lives going from one difficulty to another, into jail and out of it, only to return to it again. It appears they feel they are losers. Most come from broken families and homes where violence is a part of everyday life, and where family members have very little education. Many offenders must cope with divorce while still behind bars. Few marriages survive a prison incarceration term. Also, recidivism among men who as children grew up in families where at least one other member was a convicted offender is twelve times greater than it is for those who grew up in families where there is no criminal background. Race is also a factor in recidivism. Statistics show that Blacks are given much harsher sentences than Whites. The former also receive a much smaller percentage of probation that Whites and twice the percentage of prison sentences. Black recidivists also start their criminal records at a much younger age than other criminals and usually come from larger cities.

People in large cities, particularly Blacks, tend not to want to get involved, so they report less crime even if they do know the facts. There is also less fear by the Black potential offender of being caught if he comes from a large city. "Crime is easier than making it as an ex-offender," a three-time loser says. Something must be done to change this. These disturbing statistics reflect little credit on the system. The grinding arms of the law are doing little for the recidivist. They are only using a lot of money, most of which is wasted. The hardened offender does not develop overnight; generally he has history of repeated misdemeanor and petty offense violations. At the initial stage of a criminal career there should be reason to hope for successful reintegration efforts. We have recidivists because we do not teach them how to deal with their return to the urban community.

The responsibility lies in the hands of officials and agencies that handle these people once they are arrested and who determine how soon, and under what conditions, these criminals will be returned to the communities from which they came. Probation is one form of reintegration. A growing number of judges believe that the purpose of the prison is to rehabilitate; and that they have failed at this, and that a criminal kept out of jail has at least as good or a better chance to stop committing crime as one sent away. Surprisingly, there is some evidence to support this. In a recent review of the studies of persons on probation, it was concluded that they all indicate that offenders who have received probation generally have significantly lower rates of recidivism than those who have been incarcerated.

Furthermore, of those who are incarcerated, those receiving shorter sentences are somewhat less likely to become repeaters than those who have received longer sentences.

What we do with first offenders is probably far less important than what we do with habitual offenders. A genuine first offender is in all likelihood a young person who, in the majority of cases, will stop stealing when he gets older. Not every criminal can be released on parole, though; and what then? Many of our prison institutions are decrepit, unsafe, and overcrowded. The offenders are in some kind of need; otherwise they wouldn't have committed crimes in the first place. The need may be skills, job contacts, counseling, or education. Reintegration seeks to alter the dynamics of the offender. It seeks to decrease his need to commit acquisitive crimes by increasing his ability to secure employment; it seeks to reduce his desire to commit certain crimes by redirecting his value system; it seeks to increase his control over antisocial needs and desires by restructuring his personality. Reintegration cannot be forced on offenders, though; they must be encouraged to have the desire to change. Psychotherapy by prison therapists and group and individual counseling have all brought positive results in the reintegration process. Among offenders in prisons counseling must also lead to the solution of immediate problems.

Offenders working inside the prison is a program which offers speedier reintegration, reduced prison costs, and ready labor for seasonal and marginal jobs. At one time these programs were only available to low-risk inmates employed outside the prison on work release. New jobs are being brought into the prisons so all offenders, even high security risks, may learn the discipline of paid work and save money for their release. Those offenders earning money must pay towards their room and board, which also helps the taxpayers. This further helps to teach the offenders responsibility and self-esteem. An offender must get up in the morning, show up for work on time, and take instructions from a supervisor. If he can't cope, he's fired. Prison reformers have claimed that the only way to learn how to make a good decision is to practice. Only by letting the offenders make decisions, under supervision, will they ever learn. With everyone working in a prison, costs could decrease as much as fifty or sixty percent. The United States has very rarely used this system in the past and is just recently beginning to see its benefits. Canada has used this program with much success. This program also helps men, when they get back to the outside world, to find jobs and use their prison job skills. A study was conducted using 432 prisoners. Half received $60.00 a week and the other half received nothing. By the end of the first year, the financially aided group showed a much lower recidivism rate than the other group. Just this $60.00 wage offered the offender a source of security and self-worth. Offenders must be busy with fully, productive days; if they are not, how can we expect them to lead full, productive lives when they leave the prison grounds?

This writer believes that the most effective reintegration involves pre-sentencing intervention. In such a program, post-prison employment is already set up before the offender even leaves the courtroom to begin his sentence. While in prison, he is involved in vocational and educational programs to prepare him for his new life and job outside of prison. This program has already been effectively tested in several states.

Education is one of the most important tools to aid reintegration. Many offenders have given up hope because of their lack of education. One Black offender said to this writer, "I feel that if prisoners had been given a proper education when they were younger, many would not be in prison today." But more important than book education is the need for these prisoners to be educated in the ways of life. This offender explained, "We need to be taught about decisions, right decisions versus wrong decisions and the consequences of each. We need to be shown and taught about self-control, self-worth, character, and self motivation." For the past ten years the author has been testing this theory of combination education with maximum security offenders; this has resulted, it is believed, in offenders who are "wiser, stronger, and better prepared to reenter society."

There are still other problems that must be addressed is we are to have effective reintegration in the prisons. Better personnel are needed to run the prisons and the reintegration programs. Instead of hard, uncaring staffs, prisons need impartial, friendly and caring ones.   Offenders need to be located in a prison that is within reasonable distance of their homes, so that families and friends may come and visit them. When prisoners lose all contact with family, it is no wonder they return to prison after being released. Many times they have nowhere to call "home" but the prisons. Overcrowding is also a problem. The whole concept of reintegration depends on the offender regaining self-dignity. This is almost impossible in our large, overcrowded state facilities, where many offenders are said to become better criminals after they leave. It is very crucial that offenders be treated fairly. When they are not treated fairly while they are behind bars, we cannot expect them to treat other fairly when they are released.

If recidivism really is the criterion for success or failure, then our prisons are failing. However, the rate of recidivism can be reduced with good reintegration programs provided by caring prison staff people. We need to educate offenders, but we need to educate them not only to read and write, but to think, to decide, and to accomplish. If we do this, for many, life will no longer be a one-way street with a dead end.

THE ROLE OF THE PRISON THERAPIST IN OFFENDERS' TREATMENT AND REINTEGRATION

The role of the therapist (psychologist, counselor, social worker, etc.) can be given a simple definition: Those expectations and directives for behaviors connected with the improvement of offenders' status in the prison system. It is hoped this definition will become clearer later on in the discussion. As can be readily seen, this so-called simple definition covers a lot of ground. Expectations and directives do not originate out of this air. They originate from prison groups, each with various experiences, often conflicting demands, and a set of standards for desired behavior. It is precisely for these reasons that the role of the therapist is a continuously emerging and plightful one. White therapists are faced with pressures created by the formal organization, the prison, and by the unique characteristics of the community and the history which interact to form the total set of expectations determining their pressures in addition to many others. The Black therapist is expected to answer and be on his or her prison grounds because, in most instances, they--the prisoners, not the central prison system administration--created the pressure to have them there in the first place. Once employed, the therapist is faced with a tremendous amount of stress and strain; not only form the Non-White offender groups whose perceptions, expectations, and desired behavior may vary anywhere from North European to West African and back again, to Pan-Africanism, to Black Nationalism, to La Raza's needs and demands; but from Whites--staff and inmates-- who may be suspicious, resentful, or mistrusting as well.

It has been this author's experience that the role and expectations of the therapist can best be understood by taking into account the Black offenders' struggles for the programs the therapists are expected to originate, implement, and administer on their behalf.

Due to internal unrest during the second half of the 1970's, the nation's prison systems found themselves suddenly placed under great pressure to give dramatic demonstration that they were, in reality, committed to social justice. These pressures came from a variety of sources, including the impact of court decisions and acts of legislation.

Many prison and/or correctional systems throughout the Midwest, the West, and the East, had for some time been pursuing--in a leisurely and good-natured fashion--the goal of "better race relations" based on "equity." By the middle 1970's, the sweep of events began to dictate a quicker timetable, to demand affirmative effort far beyond that which most prison systems had as yet exerted. As the decade ended, the tempo of history had accelerated. Prison offenders' protests and prison unrest (something more than polite petitioning) occurred on various prison grounds between 1968 and 1985. Although other issues, such as the Vietnam War or parietal rules, were often present, most of those prison incidents were sparked by the issue of "Black recognition" in one form or another.

Many current reports show the tactics and strategies of prison offenders protesting over these issues of "Black recognition" on prison grounds range all the way from peaceful demonstration to prison disruption. The reaction from prison administrators and civil authorities range from eager capitulation to violent repression involving deaths.

Offenders' demands and expectations in the early seventies for relevant change in prison programs brought to prison grounds a new dimension in administrative structure. The therapist in the prison system is relatively new. Certainly only a small number of prisons have initiated a well-developed program of psychological treatment services directed at reintegration before 1975 for Black offenders on their grounds. During the 1970's this writer had the opportunity to visit, as a psychologist, prison and correctional institutions that had recognized their dilemmas and were attempting to develop mental health staff, correctional officers, and counselor offenders to deal effectively with problems caused by race within the prisons.

Given the desired behavior of offenders, a closer look at the functions which the therapist is expected to perform would indicate that the institutions create these separate therapeutic positions when some or all of the following conditions are present:
1. Black offenders demands for prison changes;

2. Interracial problems and tensions mount and multiply;

3. Prison offender groups, staff, and civil rights groups press for substantive changes in the prison system;

4. The percentage of Black offenders sharply increases;

5. The Black community becomes impatient and militant;

6. The instructional program is alleged to be irrelevant to the clientele served;

7. The staff gets out of touch with the changing requirements of the offenders served;

8. A communications gap widens between the prison system, offender and community groups;

9. The institution receives adverse publicity on race and
   prison conditions;
10. A need for expertise in the promotion of better race re-
    lated problem solving and relations among all compo-
    nents in the prison corrective process becomes evident.

As mentioned earlier, the therapist is employed to work in this area
and generally is charged with the prime responsibility--and expected--
to improve the affairs related to Black and minority offender status
in the prison system. It is difficult to ascertain a complete meaning
of the term minority affairs. In its broadest sense, it encompasses the
full range of person-to-person relations and is not restricted to
interaction between racial or ethnic groups. Nevertheless, a careful
examination of job content of the position in many prison systems
reveals a heavy emphasis on interracial problems and relationships.
The prime importance of this particular area of responsibility,
especially in the early stages of development of the therapeutic
position, may account for this emphasis in part.

Therapists are able to do their work more effectively if certain
facilitating forces are present. On the other hand, if the number of
barriers is excessive, the degree of job accomplishment is obviously
reduced.

One of the most important facilitating forces is having the full
support of the central administration staff. Another is the opportunity to go directly to the prison superintendent without having to go
through administrative layers in the organizational structure. The
sensitivity of most problems in Black minority affairs makes this
direct accessibility extremely important.

A second facilitating force is broad community awareness of the
nature and significance of Black minority problems and broad
participation in the solutions. More contact with the Black community and other communities is extremely important.

A third expediting force is a good working relationship with community groups, particularly those which are vitally concerned with the
area of Black offender reintegration processes. This especially means
an easy relationship between the total professional staff, offenders

and the communities is of the highest importance. The staff should understand the mission of the programs and recognize that it offers services that can facilitate the work of the therapist and other professional personnel. Opportunity to work directly with offenders is equally important. Efforts of the therapist can be multiplied if he has an opportunity to work through the medical-mental health-educational staff, itself, in promoting better working relationships for the Black offender as well as other offenders on prison grounds.

A concerned central prison administration staff can be a fourth facilitating force. Both financial and moral support are vitally necessary. It is most helpful for the superintendent of the prison to allow the therapist to appear before the administrative staff and the parole board to make progress reports, to interpret the thrust of therapeutic activities, and to identify problems that will require the understanding and tangible support of the total prison administrative system. A sensitive staff of a core of able associates who can initiate and carry out the mission of patient treatment and reintegration are greatly to be desired. As therapeutic treatment and reintegration are relatively new functions in the family of mental health administrative and supervisory services in prison systems, the more fully its mission is understood and accepted by the staff, the greater the opportunity for fulfillment of this mission. The promotion of good therapeutic programs depends upon a mechanism for --and a program of--good communications. This applies not only to the internal organization of the prison system, but also to resources beyond the borders of the system.

The opportunity to participate more meaningfully in the decision making process is an additional facilitating factor. This is particularly important when high-level policy decisions are made.

The following are among the barriers tending to hamper the efforts of the prison therapist:

*   Apathy: Either in the prison community or within
      the correctional system, apathy is a barrier. In
      some instances it is as devastating as hostility.

* Small budget: An inadequate budget is a constraining factor. Excessive reliance on federal funds to support the therapeutic programs is a handicap. A measure of the commitment of the prison system to an effective race and prison program is the amount of the budget which comes from local funds.

* Insufficient staff: Frequently the work load, even in the early stages of the development of the psychologist office, is too heavy for the size of the staff. Duties and responsibilities tend to multiply faster than the resources to meet them.

* Foot dragging: Sometimes there are considerable "bureaucratic delays" among prison staff in individual units or departments in cooperating with the Black therapist. This becomes a constraint in the promotion of an effective race and prison program on prison grounds.

* Racist attitudes: Hostile attitudes of a racial nature among staff members very likely will create significant barriers to the work of the therapist in the prison system.

* Extraneous assignments: To the extent that an inordinate load of so-called "extraneous assignments" is assigned to the Black therapist and robs him of valuable time and energy to devote to the main function for which he was appointed. It is possible, however, that his own definition of an "extraneous assignment" and that of the supervisor who gives him the assignment may differ.

* Putting out the fires: An excessive emphasis on emergency-type problems also robs the therapist of time to fulfill the main purpose of the department treatment and reintegration mission.

*   Limitation in decision making: If the Black
         therapist has very limited opportunity to partici-
         pate meaningfully in decision making, he may find
         this to be a significant barrier in carrying out his
         duties and meeting his responsibilities.

*   Discriminatory decision on retention: A therapist
         must carry out his or her assigned therapeutic
         duties, participate in community service, and
         publish in order to gain promotion, tenure, and
         retention. Therapists who complete all the re-
         quired activities and even go beyond that expect-
         ed of their White colleagues find that they are
         denied promotion, tenure, and retention.

After experiencing all of the above barriers--and particularly the
latter--the therapist may be so demoralized, or even angry, that his
value as a therapist is diminished; in fact, his attitude may be a
further barrier in the process of reintegrating Black offenders.
Prisons which are sincerely interested in effective change, therefore,
will have to promote therapists to positions of appropriate authority,
positions of leadership and significant decision making responsibility.
It will also be necessary to increase allocations from local funds,
augment the office staff, and utilize more people in staff positions.
Moreover, an increase in participation at developmental stages,
broader involvement with general staff, and intensified communication with the community--Black, White, and other--on the part of
the therapist is recommended.

As more local funds are committed to the support of the race and
prison programs and less reliance is placed on primarily federal
funding sources, the status of these programs will be enhanced.
Additional local support evidences a deeper commitment to the
importance of the function. If and when this change becomes more
widespread, an additional barrier to effective operation will have been
removed. Another barrier that needs removing is indifference or
lethargy on the part of many prison staff members and administrators
of the prison system.   Increased awareness of the problems of
potential and actual racial discord is needed. Lack of prison staff and
administration cultural education in racial problems and solutions is

another barrier that impedes the work of the therapist. Very substantial programs for administration and faculty education in multicultural education are called for.

Conceptually, the newly proposed role of the therapist could put into motion the wheels of treatment intervention, reintegration coordination, and communication, bridging those gaps where the cause-effect relationship between prison/correction trends and institutional transition appear to be a hindrance to offenders' achievement. The proposed aims of role model, as described above, will enable the therapist to be effective in his work and meet various audience expectations, as discussed earlier. It is also strongly felt that a system which assigns persons to positions and roles absolutely lacking in power, whether economic, social, or political, systematically produces dependent and emotionally disabled persons who lack mastery over reality problems and are important in terms of their ability to cope with life stresses. That system is therefore pathogenic and consequently will provide little positive benefit in attempting to meet current demands for institutional change on the part of the offenders--particularly Black offenders--unless the suggested strategy is adopted. Also, in those instances where the Black therapist is obliged to perform "menial" functions and responsibilities, his efforts to meet the principal thrust of this role are diluted. The removal of extraneous portions of his position presumably will help to overcome this operational barrier.

In general, the proposed role of the therapist in prison systems' programs needs to be broader and deeper. While the troubleshooting aspects of the position cannot be eliminated, time is needed to concentrate to a greater degree on preventive efforts, including:

- More direct involvement in therapeutic treatment and re-integration development and its process;

- More intensive in-service education;

- More liaison work with community groups;

- More direct participation in cabinet-level decision making;

- More advisement and counseling services for top-level administrators and heads of prison departments and other units.

Prison systems provide the crucible in which the estrangement of offenders and other social groups must be reconciled.

As proposed, organized programs in race and prison, under trained and sensitive specialists, it is believed, can ameliorate these current tensions. The proposed role and programs must be implemented and strengthened in order to increase multicultural understanding, to foster greater unity of social purpose among individuals and groups, and to facilitate the thrust for a deeper sense of personal worth on the part of those striving to establish their identity and freedom. So, in the future, the problem becomes one of the therapist dealing with the human problems of a human organization.

CHAPTER SIX

POSTSCRIPT: Treatment Perspective - Adaptive Coping

It is assumed as previously mentioned that in the future the problem becomes one of the therapist dealing with human problems of a human organization. Providing this is true, therefore, more research work is needed in the area of normal adaptation and coping, 3.3., how people, in spite of enormous odds, have managed to develop and grow within informal and formal organizational settings. This is an important consideration for the inner city Blacks, as well as the Black prison population, where many Blacks, although faced with great difficulties, do just that: survive, cope, and succeed.

However, according to Myers (1987) those persons, particularly Blacks, who don't succeed and cannot survive in prison did receive harsher punishment. In two separate research traditional studies that link inequality and official responses to crime were interrated, focusing on inequality both as a property of communities where punishment occurs and as a property of punished offenders.

An analysis of Department of Corrections data on a random sample of 14,111 violent-felony/property offenders sentenced between 1976 and 1982 in Georgia supports that conceptualization of community inequality as a context that conditions differential treatment based on offender attributes and behavior. Inequality tends to foster disproportionately harsher punishment of more dangerous and socially disadvantaged offenders; however, white rather than Black offenders are at a disadvantage in counties with high racial income inequality and large black populations. Myers suggested that greater attentiveness be paid to the economic context within which sentencing occurs, and that research strategies be developed that can specify the intervening mechanisms through which community inequality operates.

There are survival skills that both Black children and Black adults possess which are not fully appreciated or understood. For instance, inner city Black youngsters, particularly those attending mixed schools, must learn the language and culture of both the street and the school, and they must be able to shift behavior on little notice in order to survive.

According to the 1988 Children's Defense Fund -

> In order to make ends meet, both parents in many households work. While this situation may solve financial problems, the two-career family has created new problems -- the most serious being young children who are left home alone after school, or during summer vacations. An estimated 6.5 million children, ages 13 and under of full-time working parents, may go totally without care during the workday.

A majority of these children are living in urban areas. They are shifting various behavioral skills for day to day survival. Unfortunately, many of these children will become the victims of the criminal justice system. However, an understanding and enhancement of their survival skills will, perhaps, allow us to keep a great many of them from becoming a part of the criminal justice programs.

Also, knowledge of such skills is important for mental health professionals from the standpoint of prognosis, treatment and planning.

Since there are very few models or theories which explain how Black offenders like inner city persons receive psychological services. The informal social network system as described in Chapter 2 will be referred upon with limited data generated from other social-psychological bases in order to enlarge upon the argument that we simply need to provide psychological services to men in prison based upon their needs and implies understanding their cultural background/lifestyles in order to begin to assist them in fulfilling their needs.

The goal of psychotherapy in the inner city, as in the prison environment, can be said to be the support and development of ego structures that can interact with the environment and extract from it what the offender or community person needs. The task of the psychologist, therefore, is to orient the offender to go beyond mere adaptation to an exiting iniquitous situation to coping by changing the situation where possible. While not all psychologists would agree with this method, it does allow the offender to develop a wide range of constructive patterns beyond simple docile acceptance.

Both offender and therapist need to recognize what can and cannot be changed in the environment. Of course it is a difficult task to mobilize people's resources in a direction which enables them to break through some of the oppressive constraints that have been imposed upon them and they impose upon themselves. It implies that both the person being treated and the therapist are in touch with the reality of the prison and/or inner city. If there is a distortion on either part, the result will be tragic.

ACUTE SITUATIONAL DISTURBANCES

The social factors previously discussed--housing, unemployment, racism, bureaucratic unresponsiveness--tend to produce a substantial number of acute situational disturbances among inner city Blacks similar to those experienced in a prison population. In fact, these transient reactions to overwhelming environment stress are probably the most frequent problems seen in inner city mental health clinics and in the prison psychologist's office.

For example, Hopes (1986:64-71) explained in a short paper on Jail Suicide Prevention: Effective Programs Can Save Lives, concluded that:

> While mental health experts are necessary in the
> development of suicide attempt predictors and
> screening/referral criteria, their most cost-effective
> role in the ongoing prevention program is limited to
> three primary areas: 1) training and consultation
> for officers and/or paraprofessional staff, 2) follow-
> up suicide assessments, and 3) if indicated, crisis
> intervention and treatment for inmates designated
> as high risk. In this type of program, there is no
> high risk. In this type of program, there is no sub-

stitute for the well-trained officer who knows how to
identify and manage the potentially suicidal inmate.

The Hamilton County Jail (Cincinnati, Ohio) study demonstrates that
suicide attempts in jails can be predicted, and cost-effective criteria
can be developed.   Even with limited resources, a jail suicide
prevention program can be developed that will save lives, time, and
money and reduce liability exposure.

Psychologists who work with inner city Blacks in prisons/ jails have
learned that it may be necessary to be more directive and active than
usual in these cases. The flowing approach can be recommended:
recognize the offender is under stress; offer a brief, concerted effort
to help relieve current suffering; set into motion other referral
networks; call the Education Department of Hospital or other
necessary units; maintain ongoing psychological intervention when
needed.

The psychologist in the prison, as in the inner city, is in a position of
power and authority, and part of his job often involves determining
how to manipulate the system in the client's best interest. Thus, if
the psychologist can make a phone call to involved units, he can
usually get results much more quickly and dramatically than if he
delegates that responsibility to a prison counselor or educator. For
10 years using this approach, the writer used to save lives while
training staff to be more observant and useful.

This contact with a humane, empathic therapist is very important
because the inner city client, like the inmate, has spent a good part
of his life dealing with dehumanizing people and agencies. If the
psychologist chooses to be a stereotype of what a psychotherapist is
supposed to be--unempathetic, nondirective, uninvolved--the client
will probably fail to respond.

The goal of intervention in these acute situational disturbances often
involves helping the patient learn to recognize the realities of the
environment so that these realities can become more manageable.
This helps to avoid similar problems in the future.

DIAGNOSTIC ABUSE

Only one fact stands out in the statistical studies of mental disorders in Blacks as compared to Whites in prison and that is the greater number of Blacks with organic psychosis. No such differences appear in relation to manic-depressive or schizophrenic disorders, when the data are examined on the basis of symptoms rather than diagnosis. The proof of this finding lies in this writer's examination of other psychologists' and therapists' psychological reports over a ten year period. This surprising fact reveals that, despite the greater hardships facing inner city and prison Blacks, the incidence of functional psychosis is no higher than in other groups.

Monahan and Steadman (1984) attempted to make this point very clear. Discussing in their paper "Crime and Disorder," these researchers said in brief that it is widely assumed that crime and mental illness are closely linked. This intuitive assumption has influenced public policy in a number of ways. In recent years, for example, it has led some policymakers to conclude that the shift away from the hospital confinement of the mentally ill has had a substantial impact on the growth of prison populations, a crisis in many states.

Research can help inform the discussion of this important issue. By objectively measuring the effects of the release of the mentally ill, we can gain a clearer understanding of the results of this policy and where any impact on criminal justice has occurred.

Monahan and Steadman report on a six-state study which they conducted for the National Institute of Justice. Between 1968 and 1978, a period in which state mental hospital populations fell by two-thirds, the proportion of men with a history of mental hospitalization admitted to state prisons increased on average from 7.9 percent to 10.4 percent. In three of the six states, this percentage actually dropped.

The researchers conclude that the deinstitutionalization of state mental hospitals does not seem to have been a driving force in the dramatic increase in state prison populations. At the same time, however, their research suggests that the release of mental patients may have had more of an effect on another part of the correctional system - local jails. These results help us understand where resources need to be focused. Equally important, the painstaking analysis of available research summarized in this study helps to clear away some of the myths about the relationship between mental disorder and criminality.

Despite concerns that the mentally disordered may be prone to crime, this analysis found that the rate of crime among former mental patients does not appear to exceed that of the general population when matched for demographic factors such as age, race, and social class, and prior criminal history. Similarly, the limited evidence available suggests that serious mental disorder among inmate populations does not appear to be more prevalent than it is in populations of similar class in the community.

In other words, it appears that the relationship between crime and mental illness has more to do with demographic factors, age, gender, race, social class, life history, than with any direct casual link. It should be emphasized, however, that these findings refer to the relationship between crime and mental disorder in various groups, not individuals. Obviously, there are individuals who are both mentally ill and criminal and are a serious threat to potential victims.

Unless we do a better job distinguishing among the mentally ill, we do a disservice to those recovering from mental illness or whose mental health problems pose no risk to others. And we risk obscuring the real issue: criminal conduct and the threat to victims.

It is a known fact among professional therapists that schizophrenia is definitely diagnosed more often among inner city Blacks than, for example, suburban Whites. The same is true for character disorders. Neurotic conflicts, on the other hand, are rarely diagnosed in prison and inner city Blacks, and it is assumed that such clients do not respond as well to traditional psychotherapy as do White middle class neurotics.

This problem represents a number of cross-cultural issues. In neurotic conflicts, for example, psychologists have been trained to expect a series of words describing both feelings and thoughts as the presentation of neurosis. In the absence of that, character disorders are often diagnosed, particularly when the neurotic conflict leads to action or when the emotion is more directly expressed rather than verbalized.

Young Black men with emotional problems, who have some street savvy, speak some slang, and who do not openly respond to the first psychologist they see, are often avoided by being classified as having character disorders, or, more specifically, as sociopaths. Such diagnosis may be used as an excuse not to offer needed help because clients in these diagnostic categories, goes the myth, don't do well in treatment and can be forgotten or avoided.

Although neurotic conflict may lead to direct action in the inner city, as in prison, it can be treated with the traditional tools of psychotherapy --- if it is properly diagnosed.

INNER CITY BLACKS AS PRISON CLIENTS

The concept of the inner city client--nonintrospective, nonintellectual, nonverbal, impulse-ridden, unable to delay gratification--is a distortion of reality. Despite current widespread beliefs to the contrary, a large number of inner city Black inmates are able to benefit from an intrapsychically and dynamically oriented approach to therapy.

Psychologists working with inner city Blacks in prison have found that a good place to start is to educate the client as to what the process of therapy is all about. This requires discussions about the limits of both client and therapist, what can be accomplished, who can and cannot be influenced, and what reasonably can be expected. After this initial foundation is laid, client and therapist can begin to work out some reasonable goals, and, at intervals, review the progress made toward them.

A brief study developed in Scotland by McInaas and McClintock [1984] focused on the relationship between Criminal Justice and the identification and control or treatment of the mentally abnormal offenders. They were able to discover specific ways to tell if an alleged offender is suffering from a mental disorder that requires special treatment; and second, to give background information for making improvements in legal and medical services. These two points are very interesting because unless the therapist is able to control the treatment process, how else is he or she able to work effectively with the prison client or staff in that manner which will enhance psychological growth on the part of both therapist and offender.

Unfortunately, the dilemma of prison clinics is that there are too many offenders and too few therapist who can help them. Prison psychologists, then, are placed in the difficult situation or providing services with an inadequate amount of competently trained manpower. Much like the school psychologists who may have come into contact with these individuals when they were children, most prison psychologists all-too-often are satisfied with diagnosing the problem, never getting an opportunity to treat it.

Group psychotherapy has been one effective method of spreading psychological manpower throughout the prison, thereby reaching a larger number of offenders. Inner city Blacks in prison, as well as other clients, seem to respond well to this type of intervention. The use of mental health aides has also greatly increased the availability of psychological services.

Another useful method has been contractually time-limited therapy, in which the client and therapist agree to meet for ten sessions. Results can be accomplished in two ways, either by goal-oriented therapy or through an open-end dynamic contact limited only in terms of hours. Just ten contacts with a warm, empathic, caring, skilled therapist can have a significant influence.

As we are aware, the Black mental health professional is a relative newcomer to the field, and the scarcity of studies is related to this fact. Of the studies that do exist, "these few studies clearly indicate that race of the therapist influences the dynamics of the psychotherapy relationship" [Willis, 1987]. The issue is status contradiction. The White client sees the Black therapist as having high status because of his professional role, but low status because of his membership in the Black group. The Black therapist has to deal with ingrained social attitudes that the Black therapist is inferior. Some Whites respond

78   Clyde E. DeBerry

by refusing treatment while others simply drop out of treatment before really getting started. If they do continue in treatment they may resist a therapeutic alliance. They may express anger by acting superior or by challenging the therapist's credentials and interpretations, downgrading the therapists or assuming a patronizing stance.

Even with these findings and techniques, the hard fact remains that most prison clinics are painfully understaffed and are unable to provide adequate services. It would help if more sensitive psychologists would participate in prison programs, at least on a part-time basis.

PSYCHOLOGICAL HANG-UPS

As mentioned above, from the perspective of the prison mental health clinic, one of the problems with current psychological training is that there is little emphasis on the cultural differences between clients. The psychologist who is going to treat a Black person from the inner city must, among other things, learn another language. It is the language of the street, with different meanings for words and different sentence structures, and it must be learned in order to communicate with the client and to carry out meaningful therapy.

Another problem is attitudes. When young psychologists or counselors begin to work in prison clinics, they often assume that when they don't understand something it is because the client is inferior or inadequate. They seldom, if ever, assume the lack of understanding is due to some inadequacy on their part. This becomes a necessary but sometimes painful lesson to learn. Willis [1987] has made these points quite clearly.

The problem is not limited to young, inexperienced treatment specialists. There are immediate countertransference issues on the part of probably every White treatment specialist who seeks Black clients. Some research has shown that race and social class of the client and therapist, as well as training and background of the therapist, will effect the understanding and depth of how well the client does self-exploration during a therapeutic session. White therapists have a better understanding of White clients, and Black therapists have a better understanding of Black clients. Clients tend to explore deeper into themselves when involved with a therapist of the same racial background. Willis [1987] speaks of an unexplored racial attitude in which if the therapist's frame of reference, the effective development of the helping process will be blocked. He emphasized the fact that effectiveness is not based on race but on the quantity and quality of client's responses and interpersonal skills of the therapist. Training or a lack of it can be the most critical source determining the performance of the therapist in the helping relationship. A therapist with a high level of skill and functioning can attend to the differences and neutralize the effects to the extent that race will not be a critical variable. This means the psychologist must examine his own attitudes, beliefs and feelings toward Blacks before he can adequately evaluate the client, assess the problem and attempt diagnosis and treatment. Since most Blacks will continue to be treated by White treatment specialists, it becomes very important and necessary to be aware of these countertransference issues.

The issue of race should be brought out early in the treatment and should be discussed openly and honestly. It can aid in building a strong therapeutic alliance. In fact, if the therapist and client collude to maintain silence, therapeutic alliance may never develop. In order to be effective as a therapist, the White treatment specialist has to understanding the client as a Black person living in a White society. This may be the starting point of meaningful therapy.

Several traps, however, exist along the road to meaningful therapy with Black clients: The inability of some psychologists to confront their anxieties and racial differences, the blotting out of a client's Blackness, which serves to deny a significant portion of the client's identity: and finally, the defense of allowing the client to become a symbol of "Blackness", which can lead to patterned responses and stereotypic therapy.

A LOOK TO THE FUTURE: A New Beginning

Prevention of mental health problems needs to begin at the source of the difficulty. For inner city Blacks in prison a major source of the problem is White racism, the elimination of which must come from the White community. In other words, the White community must be able to understand Black problems, Black strengths and weaknesses, and Black culture, and it must also move away from the patterns of discriminatory behavior which have developed over the past 200 years.

Prevention must come from all aspects of society. Certainly the health professionals must participate, but other institutions must also be receptive to Black people. The psychologist's role in prevention efforts is that of a consultant to programs from other disciplines.

When major institutions in the wider society are open and responsive, when they incorporate Black Americans and are sensitive to the Black experience, and when they have reversed the historical practice of both mental and physical exclusion, a program of prevention of racism-induced, stress related disorders will truly have begun.

There are areas, however, where initiative and responsibility rest with Black people themselves. Blacks must take the initiative for building up Black communities and for making them fulfill the needs of Black people. As White people work on racist attitudes, Blacks must begin to redefine themselves and must not accept the negative definitions that have been handed down from one generation to the next. Finally, leadership must come from within the Black community and not from outside it, and that leadership must be willing to work with the White community to build up Black institutions and power.

For psychological professionals, the goal should be a willingness to work in partnership with other disciplines and institutions to develop creative approaches to the problems that have been touched upon. Also of importance is an increased sensitivity to Black people on the part of White psychologists, particularly since the number of White practitioners will always exceed the number of Black practitioners.

CHAPTER SEVEN

SOCIAL IMPLICATIONS FOR PRISON CHANGE

A detailed comparison of this study with nationwide data and studies of other prison systems would consume another large volume. With all confidence it can be stated that offenders who have developed satisfactory network systems would be more prepared for release and less likely to continue to engage in criminal behavior. Prison officials, therapists, parole boards, etc., should take this implication into consideration in making responsible decisions concerning release.

Based on the research found in this dissertation, we feel that offenders who had contact with friends and relatives, demonstrated the ability to get along with other people, belonged to organizations, planned goals, discussed personal problems with the treatment staff, and sought personal counseling demonstrated more coping skills. Therefore, it is predicted that they would be the least likely to return to the prison environment. However, as previously stated, it must be understood that this writer provided an environment as well as psychological services for these offenders.

As mentioned earlier, the therapist must be committed, concerned, and must maintain a high level of interest in his or her clients. The therapist must understand the importance of social networking and must encourage the offender to participate in such. If nothing else, for their own self interest. Since completing this study, this writer has been in contact with the institution where the study originated. Reports from the staff and the inmates show that the individuals who participated in this study and who have, since the time of this study, been released have demonstrated to ability to maintain employment, have kept in contact with family and friends, have become avid churchgoers, and have maintained membership in local organizations which have a prison based interest. Again, these are not results of a scientific study, they merely reflect this writer's experiences.

It is seriously encouraged that other social and behavioral scientists duplicate this study and discuss these issues to discover the influence of social networking in hopes that over a period of time there will be a decrease in criminal behavior and no need for Blacks in corrections.

APPENDICES A

PSYCHOLOGICAL ASSESSMENT OF RESIDENTIAL OFFENDERS

In an effort to better assess the needs of residents assigned to K-Dormitory, this questionnaire has been developed to gather needed information.

The first part of the questionnaire is designed to gather facts that will assist in the development of future programs, with the second part asking for opinions on different subject matters. Please answer all questions to the best of your ability.

1. Sex:

a. Male _____

2. What was your age at your last birthday?

a.	18 or under	_____
b.	19-25	_____
c.	26-35	_____
d.	36-45	_____
e.	45 or older	_____

3. What is the nature of your offense? (Fill in)

a.	Class A	_____
b.	Class B	_____
c.	Class C	_____
d.	Class D	_____

4. Marital Status:

a.	Single	_____
b.	Married	_____
c.	Separated	_____

d. Divorced   ____
e. Widowed   ____

5. Ethnic Group:

   a. Black-American   ____
   b. Oriental   ____
   c. Native American   ____
   d. Spanish speaking   ____
      (Chicano, Latino, Puerto Rican, or Cuban)
   e. White-American   ____

6. In which size community did you live before you came to the Indiana State Prison?

   a. Farm   ____
   b. Village, 250-2,499 population   ____
   c. Town, 2,500-24,999 population   ____
   d. City, 25,000-99,000 population   ____
   e. City, over 100,000 population   ____

7. What was the educational background of your father?

   a. Did not finish high school   ____
   b. High school graduate   ____
   c. College, but did not finish   ____
   d. College graduate   ____
   e. Professional or graduate degree   ____

8. What is your church affiliation?

   a. Roman Catholic   ____
   b. Protestant   ____
   c. Jewish   ____
   d. Moslem   ____
   e. Other   ____

9. Hobbies/interests   _____
   _____

10. Date of recent Psychological Test _____

11. About how often were you on the telephone with close friends or relatives during the past month? (Check one)

    a. Every day   _____
    b. Several times a week   _____
    c. About once a week   _____
    d. 2 or 3 times a week   _____
    e. Not at all   _____

12. In general, how well are you getting along with other people these days? (Check one)

    a. Better than usual   _____
    b. About the same   _____
    c. Not as well as usual   _____

13. How often have you attended a religious service during the past month? (Check one)

    a. Every day   _____
    b. More than one a week   _____
    c. 2 or 3 times in past month _____
    d. Once in past month   _____
    e. Not at all in past month _____

14. What kinds of volunteer groups or organizations do you belong to or attend (Please check)

    1. Jaycees Organization   _____
    2. Lifers Club   _____
    3. Recreational Activities   _____
    4. Basketball League   _____
    5. Softball League   _____
    6. AMVETS   _____
    7. A.A.   _____
    8. Religious Services   _____

15. How active are you in attending these activities?

    VA =   Very active - attend most meetings
     A =   Active - attend fairly often
    NA =   Not active - hardly ever attend (Please check below)

Jaycees	VA___	A___	NA___
Lifers Club	VA___	A___	NA___
Recreational Activities	VA___	A___	NA___
Baseball League	VA___	A___	NA___
Softball League	VA___	A___	NA___
AMVETS	VA___	A___	NA___
A.A.	VA___	A___	NA___
Religious Services	VA___	A___	NA___

16. When you need assistance, how helpful are the following groups?

	Very Helpful	Helpful	Not Helpful	Expect No Help
Jaycees	___	___	___	___
Lifers Club	___	___	___	___
Recreational Activities	___	___	___	___
Baseball League	___	___	___	___
Softball League	___	___	___	___
AMVETS	___	___	___	___
A.A.	___	___	___	___
Religious Services	___	___	___	___

17. As you consider your future goals in life, which of the following is most important to you? (Check one)

    a. Obtaining a reasonably high status in the community. __
    b. Being able to help other people. ___
    c. Achieving a certain amount of power in the community.___
    d. Accumulating a sufficient amount of money to be able to live well. ___
    e. Helping to make the society a better place for people to live.
       ___

18. Do you receive help/support from your friends when you are having personal problems/feeling emotionally upset? (Please check)

A lot of help ____   Some help ____   Little help ____

No help at all ____   Don't ask for help ____

19. In general, how satisfied would you say you are with job opportunities at K-Dorm. (Check one)

Very satisfied ____   Satisfied ____   Dissatisfied ____
Very dissatisfied ____

20. In general, how satisfied would you say you are with the living arrangement at K-Dorm. (Check one)

Very satisfied ____   Satisfied ____   Dissatisfied ____
Very dissatisfied ____

21. Are you satisfied with the help you receive from friends and family?

Very satisfied ____   Satisfied ____   Dissatisfied ____
Very dissatisfied ____

22. If you were having emotional problems, which one of the following professionals would you seek for help? You may check more than one answer.

    1. Psychiatrist   ____
    2. Psychologist   ____
    3. Unit Team Members   ____
    4. Counselor   ____
    5. Correction Officer   ____
    6. Mental Health Center   ____
    7. Hospital   ____
    8. Other   ____
    9. None   ____

23. Are you having emotional problems with any of the following? (Check one)

    1. Problem with staff
    2. Problem with job placement   ___
    3. Problem with other offender   ___
    4. Problem with spouse - girlfriend   ___
    5. Problem with divorce, death of person   ___
    6. Feeling depressed   ___
    7. Feeling anxious   ___
    8. Other   ___

24. Do you feel your friends would be supportive if you decided to seek help from mental health professionals?

    Very supportive ___ Supportive ___ Unsupportive ___

    Tell me that it's stupid ___

25. How much would your friend's attitude influence your decision to seek psychological services?

    A lot of influence ___   Some influence ___

    Very little influence ___ No influence ___

26. What factors do you think influence a person's decision to seek help from mental health professionals? Check statements which apply to you.

    Realizing or knowing they have a problem   ___

    Discussing problem with friends and relatives   ___

    Knowing where to go for help   ___

    Being referred by Parole Board, Clemency Commission   ___

    Being referred by job   ___

Being referred by Counselor   ___

Being referred by Unit Team   ___

Being referred by Prison Staff   ___

27. Which of the following psychological services best fit your present needs? (Check only one)

Personal Counseling	___
Group Psychotherapy	___
Stress Management	___
Career Education	___
Drug-substance abuse	___
Interpersonal relations	___
Value Clarification	___
Human relations group	___
Marital-family counseling	___
Individual psychotherapy	___
Others	___

28. How much influence do you feel these factors have on keeping people away from psychological services? (Check each one below)

    a. Afraid people will think you to be crazy

       A lot of influence   ___   Some influence ___

       Little influence   ___   No influence   ___

    b. Fear of unfavorable attitudes from job supervisor

       A lot of influence   ___   Some influence ___

       Little influence   ___   No influence   ___

    c. Don't think they need help

       A lot of influence   ___   Some influence ___

Little influence ___   No influence ___

29. Do you believe that many K-Dorm offenders don't seek services from mental health professionals because they think they will not receive any help?

    Strongly agree ___   Agree ___   Disagree __

30. What do you see as the greatest mental health problem interfering with your development as a person since you have been on trusty status? (Check which statements apply to you)

    1. Employment assignment   ___
    2. Housing arrangement   ___
    3. Adjusting to being on trusty status   ___
    4. Interpersonal relations   ___
    5. Staff - offender relations   ___
    6. Hygiene - personal/environmental   ___
    7. Food services   ___
    8. Medical services   ___
    9. Psychological services   ___
    10. Religious services   ___
    11. Race relations   ___
    12. Recreational   ___
    13. Social Services   ___
    14. None of the above   ___

APPENDICES B

REFERENCES

Andrews, G., Tennant C., Henson, M., & Vallant, G., Life event stress, social support, coping styles and risk of psychological impairment. **Journal of Nervous and Mental Disease**, May 1978, Vol. 166 5.

Anderson, J., Religion and Black Americans. **Michigan City News Dispatch**, May 9, 1982.

Andrulis, D., Ethnicity as a variable in the Utilization and Referral Patterns of A Comprehensive Mental Health Center. **Journal of Community Psychology**, 1977, (5) 231-237.

Asser, E., Social class and help-seeking behavior. **American Journal of Community Psychology**, October 1978, 6 (5) 464-477.

Barnes, A., The black kinship system. **Pylon**, Winter 1981, 369-480.

Billingsly, A., **Black Families in White America**, Englewood Cliff, H.J. Prentic Hall, 1968.

Bissonette, R., The bartender as mental health gatekeepers: A role analysis. **Community Mental Health Journal**, 1977, 13 92-99.

Boswell, D. M., Person crisis and mobilization of social network. **Social Networks in Urban Situations**, Mitchel, J.C., (ED), Manchester University Press, 1969.

Bott, E., **Family and Social Network**, London, Tavistock Publishing, 1970.

Brooks, C., New mental health perspectives in the black community. **Social Casework**, October 1974, 469-489.

92   Clyde E. DeBerry

Brown, B., Social and psychological correlates of help-seeking behavior among urban adults. **American Journal of Community Psychology**, 1978, 6, (5) 425-441.

Calneck, M., Racial factors in the countertransference: The Black Therapist and the Black Client. **American Journal of Orthopsychiatry**, January 1970, 40 (1) 103-115.

Cannon, M., & Locke, B. Z., Being black is detrimental to one's mental health, myth or reality? **Pylon**, Winter 1977, Vol. 38, (4) 126-137.

Cobb, C., Community mental health service and the lower socioeconomic classes. **American Journal Orthopsychiatry**, April 1972, 42 (3) 404-414.

Cole, J. & Pilisk, M., Differences in provision of mental health services by race. **American Journal Orthopsychiatry**, July 1976, 46 (3) 510-525.

Davis, K. & Swartz, J., Increasing black students utilizing of mental health service. **American Journal of Orthopsychiatry**, March 1971, 43, (4), 112-118.

Dawkins, J., Terry, J., & Dawkins, M., Personality and life style factors in utilization of mental health services. **Psychological Reports**, 1980, 46, 383-386.

Dean, A., & Linn, N., Stress suffering role on social support. **The Journal of Nervous and Mental Disease**, 1977, 165 (6), 403-417.

Donald, C., & Ware, J., **The Quantification of Social Contracts and Resources**, Rand Corporation, 1982.

Dressler, W., Extended family relationships, social support and mental health in a southern black community. **Journal of Health and Social Behavior**, 1985, 26, 39-48.

Dubois, W.E.B., The function of the Negro church. **The Black Church in America**. Nelson & Nelson (ED), Basic Books, 1971, 400-416.

Eaton, W., Life events, social supports, and psychiatric symptoms. **Journal of Health and Social Behavior**, June 1978, 19, 230-238.

Finlayson, A., Social networks in coping resources. **Social Science & Medicine** 1976, (10), 97-103.

Fischer, E. & Cohn, S., Demographic correlates of attitudes toward seeking professional psychological help. **Journal of Consulting and Clinical Psychology**, 1972, 39, (1), 70-74.

Fisher, E. & Le Be., Turner, J., Orientations to seeking professional help-attitudinal scale. **Journal of Consulting and Clinical Psychology**, 1970, 35, (1), 79-90.

Fischer, J., Negroes and whites and rates of mental illness. **Psychiatry**, 1969, 34, (4), 428-446.

Frazier, E. F., **The Negro Family in the United States**, University of Chicago Press, 1939.

Frazier, E. F., **Black Bourgeoisie**, New York, McMillan Company, 1962.

Frazier, E. F., **Negro Church in America**, Schocken Books, 1963.

Gibson, A. C., Black elderly females. **Behavior Today Newsletters**, April 3, 1983.

Gourash, N., Help seeking: A review of the literature. **American Journal of Community Psychology**. (October, 1978, 6 (5), 413-425.

Gurin, G., **Americans View Their Mental Health**, New York, Basic Books, 1960.

Hallowitz, D., Counseling and treatment of poor black families. **Social Casework**, October 1975, 451-459.

Hamilton, C. B., **Black Preachers in America,** William Morrow, 1972.

Helms, J., Counseling black women. **Counseling Psychologist,** 1979, 8 (1), 40-41.

Henderson, S., The social network, support and neurosis. **American Journal of Psychiatry,** 1977, 131, 185-191.

Hill, R., **Strengths of Black Families,** National Urban League, Washington, D.C., 1972.

Horowitz, A., Social Networks and pathways to psychiatric treatment. **Social Forces,** Vol. 56, 1977, 86-105.

Isaac, S., & Michael, W., **Handbook in Research and Education,** San Diego, 1971.

Jacobson, A., et a., Factors relating to the use of mental health service. **Public Health Reports,** May-June 1978, 93 (3), 232-39.

Kadushin, C., **Why People Go to Psychiatrists,** New York Atherton, 1969.

Kammeyer, K., & Bolten, C., Community and family factors related to the use of family services agency. **Journal of Marriage and The Family,** August, 1968, 488-498.

Keefe, S., Why Mexican-Americans underutilize mental health clinics. **Family and Mental Health in the Mexican-American Community,** Casas & Keefe Editors, 1978.

Kessler, R., Stress statutes & psychological distress. **Journal of Health Social Behavior,** September, 1979.

Kerlinger, F., **Foundations of Behavioral Research,** Holt, Rinehart, and Winston, 1973.

Kliner, R., Mental disorder and status based on race. **Psychiatry,** 1960 (23) 271-75.

King, L., Social and cultural influence on psychopathology. **Annual Review of Psychology**, 1978, 29, 405-433.

Krebs, R., Some effects of a white institution on black psychiatric outpatients. **American Journal Orthopsychiatry**, July 1971, 41 (4), 589-596.

Kulka, R., Veroff, J., & Douvan E., Social class and the use of professional help for personal problems. **Journal Health and Social Behavior**, March 1976, 20, 2-17.

Ladner, J., **Tomorrow's Tomorrow**, New York Doubleday & Company, 1971.

Leavy, R., Social support and psychological disorder: A review. **Journal of Community Psychology, Vol II**, January 1983, 3-21.

Leiberman, N. & Nullan, J., Does Help Help? **American Journal of Community Psychology**, October 1978, 6 (5) 499-517.

Liebow, E., **Tally's Corner**, Canada Little Brown & Co., 1967.

Liem, R., & Liem, J., Social class and mental illness, the role of the economic stress and social support. **Journal of Health and Social Behavior**, June 1978.

Linn, N., Simone, R., Ensel, W. & Kuo. Social support and stressful life events and illness. **Journal of Health & Social Behavior**, June 1979, 108-119.

Lurie, O., Parents attitudes toward children problems and toward use of mental health services. **American Journal of Orthopsychiatry**, January 1974, 44 (1), 109-120.

McAdoo, H., Black Kinship. **Psychology Today**, May 1979, 67, 69, 70, 79, 110.

Mckinlay, J., Social networks, lay consultation and help-seeking behavior. **Social Forces**, 1973, 51, 275-292.

Malzberg, B., Mental diseases among Negroes. **Mental Hygiene,** 1959, 43, 457-459.

Mayfield, W., Mental health in the black community. **Social Work,** May 1972, 106-27.

Meneghan. E. Seeking help for parental concern in the middle years. **American Journal of Community Psychology,** October 1978, 6 (5) 477-487.

Mitchell, R., & Trickett, E., Social networks as mediators of social support. **Community Mental Health Journal,** Spring 1980, (46) 47-44.

Myrdall, G. (1944), **The Black Church in America,** Nelson & Nelson (ED), Basic Books, 1971, p. 83.

Neff, J. & Husaini, B., Race, socioeconomic status and psychiatric impairment. **Journal of Community Psychology,** 1980, 8, 16-19.

Nobles, W. A formulative and empirical study of black families, #) ED-90-C-255, Dept. Health, Education and Welfare Office of Child Development, Washington, D.C., 1975.

Padilla, A., Carlos & Keefe's Mental health service utilization by Mexican-Americans. **Psychotherapy with the Spanish Speaking: Issues in Research & Service Delivery,** Miranda-Editor, 1976.

Passmanick, B., Some misconception concerning differences in the racial prevalence of mental disease. **American Journal of Orthopsychiatry,** 1963, 33, 72-78.

Pierce, W. The comprehensive community mental health program and the black community. **Black Psychology,** R. Jones (ED), New York, Harper & Row, 1972, 398-405.

Raphael, E., Community structures and acceptance of psychiatric aid. **American Journal of Sociology,** 1964, (6), 340-58.

Raynes, A., & Warren, G., Some distinguishing features of patients filing to attend psychiatric clinic after referral. **American Journal Orthopsychiatry**, July 1971, 41 (4) 581-586.

Redlich, F. & Hollingshed, A., Social class differences in attitudes toward psychiatry. **American Journal Orthopsychiatry**, 1965, 25, 60-70.

Rosenblatt, A. & Mayer, J., Help seeking for family problems. **American Journal of Psychiatry**, 1972, (28).

Rosenthal, D. & Frank J., The fate of psychiatric clinic outpatients assigned to psychotherapy. **Journal of Nervous and Mental Disease,** 1959, 127, 330-343.

Schneider, J., et al., Ethnic group perceptions of mental health providers. **Journal of Counseling Psychology**, 1980, 27, (6), 589-596.

Schrieber, S., Glidewell, Jr., Social norms and helping in a community of limited liability. **American Journal of Community Psychology,** October 1978, (6), 441-453.

Smith, E., Mental health and service delivery systems for black females. **Journal of Black Studies**, 1981, 12 (2), 126-141.

Solomon, B., **Black Empowerment**, Columbia Press, 1976.

Stack, C. **All Our Kin**, New York, Harper & Row, 1974.

Staples, R., Black family life and development. **Mental Health: Challenge to the Black Community**, Gary L., (ED), Philadelphia Ardmore, 1978.

Sue, S., Community mental health services to minority groups. **American Psychologist**, August 1977, 616-624.

Sullivan, L., Black religion and community service. **Black Religion and Public Policy**, Washington, J., Ed. 1974.

Taber, R., A systems approach to the delivery of mental health services in black ghettos. **American Journal Orthopsychiatry**, July 1972, 40 (4) 702-709.

Thoits, P., Studying social support as a buffer against life stress. **Journal of Health and Social Behavior**, June 1982, 23, 145-159.

Tolsdorf, C., Social networks, support, and coping. **Family Process**, 1976, 15, 407-417.

Turkat, D., Social networkds: theory and practice. **Journal of Community Psychology**, 1980 (8), 99-109.

Turner, S. L., Disability among schizophrenics in a rural community: Services and social support. **Research in Nursing and Health**, 1979, 2, 151-161.

Turner, J., Social support as a contingency in psychological well-being. **Journal of Health and Social Behavior**, December 1981, 22, 357-367.

Walker, K., McBridge, A., & Vachon, M., Social support networks and crisis of bereavement. **Social Science & Medicine**, 1977, 11, 35-41.

Willie, C., The black family and social class. **American Journal of Orthopsychiatry**, 1974, 44, 50-56.

Williams, A., Ware, J., Donald, C., A model of mental health, life events, and social supports. **Journal of Health and Social Behavior**, 1981, Vol. 22, 324-336.

Windle, C., Correlates of community mental health center underservice to non-whites. **Journal of Community Psychology**, 1980, (8), 140-146.

Wolkon, G., Morwiaki, S. & Williams, J. Race and social class as factors in orientation toward psychotherapy. **Journal of Counseling Psychology**, 1973, 20, 312-316.

ABOUT THE AUTHOR

Clyde E. DeBerry is an associate professor of Criminal Justice at Grambling State University. He received a B.S. in Education at Winston Salem State University, an M.A. in Counseling and Social Sciences from Northern Arizona State University, his Ed.D. from the University of Oregon, and his Ph.D. from Columbia Pacific University. Dr. DeBerry's career experiences have expanded from the public-private, elementary-secondary school teacher to chief psychologist of the Indiana State Prison System to university teaching and research. His research and writing have focused on the problems and issues of race and education both in educational and correctional institutions. DeBerry's research interests are diverse, and he has presented and published papers on a variety of educational and criminal justice issues.

ISSUES IN AMERICAN JUSTICE LIBRARY

ALTERNATIVE SENTENCING: ELECTRONICALLY MONITORED CORREC-TIONAL SUPERVISION by Richard Enos et.al. (University of North Texas) ISBN 1-55605-218-9 (paperback), ISBN 1-55605-219-7 (hardback).

FINDING CRIMINAL JUSTICE (IN THE LIBRARY): A STUDENT MANUAL OF INFORMATION RETRIEVAL AND UTILIZATION SKILLS by Dennis C. Tucker (Indiana Cooperative Library Services Authority) and Frank Schmalleger (Pembroke State University), ISBN 1-55605-183-2 (paperback), ISBN 1-55605-184-0 (hard-back).

ISSUES IN JUSTICE: EXPLORING POLICY ISSUES IN THE CRIMINAL JUSTICE SYSTEM edited with contributions by Roslyn Muraskin (Long Island University), ISBN 1-55605-168-9 (paperback), ISBN 1-55605-169-7 (hardback).

ETHICS IN CRIMINAL JUSTICE: A JUSTICE PROFESSIONAL READER edited with contributions by Frank Schmalleger (Pembroke State University), ISBN 1-55605-118-2 (paperback), ISBN 1-55605-119-9 (hardback).

COMPUTERS IN CRIMINAL JUSTICE: ISSUES AND APPLICATIONS edited with contributions by Frank Schmalleger (Pembroke State University), ISBN 1-55605-175-1 (paperback), ISBN 1-55605-176-x (hardback).

DORMITORY DRUG DENS AND DUE PROCESS: THE LAW OF SEARCH IN THE FEDERAL SYSTEM by Walfred H. Peterson (Washington State University), ISBN 0-932269-86-9 (paperback), ISBN 0-932269-86-9H (hardback).

HANDBOOK OF BASIC TRIAL EVIDENCE: A COLLEGE INTRODUCTION by Joseph M. Pellicciotti (Indiana University), ISBN 1-55605-191-3 (paperback).

BLACKS IN THE FEDERAL JUDICIARY: NEUTRAL ARBITERS OR JUDICIAL ACTIVISTS? by Abraham L. Davis (Morehouse College), ISBN 1-55605-098-4 (paperback).

 Wyndham Hall Press

Editorial · Marketing · Shipping
52857 County Road 21
Bristol, Indiana 46507
219/848-4834